THE **MINI** ROUGH GUIDE TO
BRUGES
& GHENT

YOUR TAILOR-MADE TRIP
STARTS HERE

Tailor-made trips and unique adventures crafted by local experts

HOW ROUGHGUIDES.COM/TRIPS WORKS

STEP 1

Pick your dream destination, tell us what you want and submit an enquiry.

STEP 2

Fill in a short form to tell your local expert about you dream trip and preferences

STEP 3

Our local expert will craft your tailor-made itinerary. You'll be able to tweak and refine it until you're completely satisfied.

STEP 4

Book online with ease, pac your bags and enjoy the trip! Our local expert will b on hand 24/7 while you're on the road.

PLAN AND BOOK YOUR TRIP AT
ROUGHGUIDES.COM/TRIPS

HOW TO DOWNLOAD YOUR FREE EBOOK

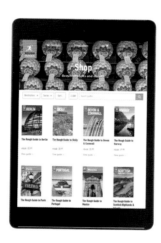

1. Visit **www.roughguides.com/ free-ebook** or scan the **QR code** opposite

2. Enter the code **bruges663**

3. Follow the simple step-by-step instructions

For troubleshooting contact: mail@roughguides.com

10 THINGS NOT TO MISS

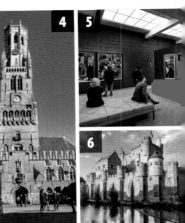

1. **THE BEGIJNHOF**
    A peaceful retreat in the heart of the city.
    See page 39.

2. **ONZE-LIEVE-VROUWEKERK**
    Bruges's finest and most important church.
    See page 35.

3. **CANALS**
    Cruising the waterways is a relaxing way to
    enjoy the historic sights. See page 117.

4. **BELL TOWER**
    The 13th-century structure looms over the
    city. See page 27.

5. **GROENINGEMUSEUM**
    Works by Flemish masters. See page 33.

6. **HET GRAVENSTEEN**
    A medieval fortress in the heart of Ghent.
    See page 75.

7. **HUIS TER BEURZE**
    An elegant 15th-century mansion.
    See page 51.

8. **STADHUIS**
    The Gothic Town Hall. See page 28.

9. **SINT-JANSHOSPITAALMUSEUM**
    Discover masterpieces by the painter Hans
    Memling in the old hospital's church.
    See page 37.

10. **BASILICA OF THE HOLY BLOOD**
    Stands guard over the holiest relic in Bruges.
    See page 30.

A PERFECT DAY

9.00am

Breakfast. For breakfast in a splendid setting, go to the delightful Blackbird café (see page 102).

10.00am

The Markt. Stroll into the nearby Markt for a turn around the magnificent market square. Take in the Belfort (belfry) and medieval buildings, then discover what 13th-century Bruges was like, inside the Historium.

11.00am

The Burg. The historic square contains the medieval Basiliek van het Heilig-Bloed, the lovely Gothic Stadhuis and the Baroque Proosdij (Provost's House).

12.30pm

Lunch. Breydel De Coninc (www.restaurant-breydel.be; see page 102) in Breidelstraat is a good traditional restaurant. For something more sophisticated, go down Blinde-Ezelstraat and cross the canal to the Vismarkt (Fish Market) for the highly regarded seafood restaurant Den Gouden Karpel (www.dengoudenkarpel.be; see page 103).

2.00pm

Groeninge. Head along the canal on photogenic Rozenhoedkaai and tree-shaded Dijver, then turn left into Groeninge. If you visit only one museum in Bruges, this should be it. The collection of paintings by medieval Flemish Primitives is world-class, including Jan van Eyck, Hans Memling, Rogier van der Weyden and Gerard David, among others.

IN BRUGES

3.00pm

Culture fix. If you fancy more culture, or you missed out on the Groeninge, cross the pretty little Boniface Bridge and continue to the Gothic Onze-Lieve-Vrouwekerk (Church of Our Lady). The church is worth visiting for its *Madonna and Child* sculpture by Michelangelo. The church's 122m (400-ft) -tall brick tower is the second-tallest of its kind in the world, and once served as an inland lighthouse for ships on their way to Bruges.

4.30pm

Towards the Begijnhof. Across the street is Sint-Janshospitaalmuseum, whose old church houses works by Hans Memling. By way of the Halve Maan brewery, you arrive at the pretty courtyard of the Unesco-listed Begijnhof.

6.00pm

The Lake of Love. Just south of the Begijnhof, the Minnewater lake can be imaginatively translated as the 'Lake of Love', though it probably takes its name from Bruges' medieval Binnen Water (Inner Harbour). On its east bank is a handsome park. Take a stroll around here and the neighbourhood by the lake's eastern shore.

8.00pm

Dinner. If you want to dine in this area, off the north end of the Minnewater you will find the traditional Flemish restaurant Maximiliaan van Oostenrijk (www.maximiliaanvanoostenrijk.be; see page 104). Alternatively, return to the Vismarkt for dinner at Huidevettershuis (www.huidevettershuis.be; see page 104), which is set within a medieval guild house.

CONTENTS

OVERVIEW   10

HISTORY AND CULTURE   12

OUT AND ABOUT   25

South from the Markt   27
The Burg 28, Around Vismarkt 32, The Groeninge Museum 33,
The Gruuthuse Museum 35, Onze-Lieve-Vrouwekerk 35, Sint-Janshospitaalmuseum 37,
Around Mariastraat 38, The Begijnhof 38, Minnewater 40, Katelijnestraat 41

West from the Markt   41
Around 't Zand Square 42

North from the Markt   46
Jan van Eyckplein 46, East of Jan van Eyckplein 48,
West of Jan van Eyckplein 51, North of Jan van Eyckplein 53

Excursions   55
Damme 55, Dudzele 57, Lissewege 57, Zeebrugge 57, De Haan 58,
Oostende (Ostend) 59, Veurne 62, Ypres and Flanders Fields 63, The War Cemeteries 65,
Sint-Andries 67, Tillegembos 67, Kasteel Loppem 67

Ghent   68
Sint-Baafskathedraal 69, The Belfort and Lakenhalle 71,
Botermarkt and Hoogpoort 71, Korenlei and Graslei 73, North of Korenlei 75,
Gravensteen 75, From Kraanlei to Vrijdagmarkt 76, Around Veldstraat 77,
Fine Arts Museums 78, Sint-Pietersplein 81

THINGS TO DO | 83

Shopping | 83
Entertainment | 87
Sports | 90
Activities for Children | 90

FOOD AND DRINK | 93

TRAVEL ESSENTIALS | 107

WHERE TO STAY | 128

INDEX | 134

HIGHLIGHTS

Easy To Explore | 10
Trade Centre | 16
Literary Revival | 18
Historical Landmarks | 23
Lacemaking | 49
The Coast Tram | 59
Tours of Remembrance | 64
Who Painted the Alterpiece? | 68
How Flanders Influenced Art | 80
Calendar of Events | 92
Belgian Beers | 100

OVERVIEW

For hundreds of years Belgium has been coveted, invaded and fought over by Europe's great powers. Steeped in history and legend, the country was the site of numerous bloody battles, particularly in the northern region of Flanders. Once ignored in favour of other holiday destinations, Belgium's charm is no longer a secret and its historic towns, first-class museums, hearty food, rich beers and ancient architecture are well-known. Most beautiful of all these attractions is Bruges, Europe's best-preserved medieval city and the capital of West Flanders, one of Belgium's 11 provinces. Its gabled houses, meandering canals, and narrow pedestrianized cobblestone streets combine to create one of Europe's most romantic towns.

Bruges' egg-shaped historic centre is contained by a 7km (4.3-mile) -long 'ring canal', which traces the route of the former defensive outer ramparts. A ring road follows this perimeter boundary and, along with other restrictions, keeps most traffic away from the centre.

The city's history is evident everywhere; in its streets and buildings, its art, culture and festivals. Bruges is so picturesque that it is hard to imagine the filth, dirt and disease that would have been

EASY TO EXPLORE

Belgium is a compact country (less than 280km/174 miles across at its widest point), so nowhere is very far away. Most of the excursions in this guide are within a few miles of Bruges or Ghent, themselves connected by a reliable half-hour train journey. Those a little farther away are still easily accessible, thanks to the country's superb railways.

a standard part of life here in the Middle Ages. It has an effortless charm that casts its spell on visitors almost immediately, thanks to its compact geography, easily explored on foot, by bike, or even on the water.

Water long formed an important part of the landscape and economy of Bruges. Canals linked the city to the coast and important industrial centres in Belgium and around Europe. A leisurely cruise along the canals is still an experience

View from Rozenhoedkaai

not to be missed, and one of the best ways of viewing the wonderful cityscape.

Eating and drinking are mostly hearty events and form an important part of life. Belgian cuisine is justly famous throughout the world, both for its quality and its quantity, and there are plenty of fine restaurants in Bruges. An intrinsic part of everyday eating is the Belgian French fry *(friet)*, which is available everywhere, and often eaten with mayonnaise. Equally ubiquitous are the exquisite Belgian chocolates you will see in mouth-watering shop displays.

The Flemish have a strong sense of pride in their history and achievements. Bruges had a distinctive role in the development of its region. Before the foundation of the Belgian state in 1830, Bruges was virtually an autonomous city-state. Nationhood itself is a fiercely debated issue in Belgium. Bruges is part of Flanders, where the official language is Dutch, but a large proportion of the country is inhabited by French-speaking Walloons.

HISTORY AND CULTURE

Bruges has a very long and distinguished history, which considerably predates Belgium's foundation in 1830. Inhabited since Neolithic times, the region's story really begins with the Belgae, a Gallo-Germanic tribe living in northern Gaul. In the first of many centuries of occupations, Julius Caesar's legions successfully invaded Belgae territory in 57 BC.

THE KINGDOM OF THE FRANKS

The Romans withdrew from Gaul in the 5th century as the Roman Empire went into decline. Bruges may have been a minor Gallo-Roman port protected against Germanic sea-raiders by a *castellum* (fort). Much of Gaul succumbed to the Franks, who had been settling in the region for the previous two centuries. They founded their Merovingian kingdom around Tournai in the south of today's Belgium, while to the north and east the region was divided between Franks, Frisians and Saxons. The conversion to Christianity of the Frankish King Clovis in 498 led to a gradual northward spread of the new faith, which eventually converted the entire region.

A 15th-century painting of a Bruges goldsmith in his shop

In 768, the Frankish king Charlemagne set about establishing a unified kingdom in this part of western Europe. By military and diplomatic means he expanded his influence, culminating in his coronation by the Pope in 800 as the Holy Roman Emperor. On his death in 814, the empire passed to his son Louis, and on Louis' death in 840 was divided between his three sons. The division left a narrow strip of Europe, including the Low Countries (Belgium, Luxembourg and the Netherlands), sandwiched between French- and German-speaking tribes.

Early record

The first recorded mention of Bruges dates from the 8th century AD, though little is known about the town's origins, except that the name possibly comes from the Vikings.

THE GOLDEN AGE OF BRUGES

Flanders, including Bruges, came under the nominal rule of a succession of German and French kings, but real power was in the hands of local nobles, who tried to weaken the authority of the French and German feudal kingdoms. Some of these lords were wealthier than their rulers and negotiated charters of autonomous rights for towns in exchange for taxes and military assistance.

Bruges began to emerge from the prehistoric soup around the mid-7th century, when St Eligius preached in coastal Flanders. Chronicles of his life refer to a Frankish community called the Municipium Flandrense, which seems to have been Bruges. The first certain mention of Bruges occurs in 851 in records of monks from Ghent and by 864 the word 'Bruggia' appears on coins of Charles the Bald, king of the West Franks, to whom Flanders owed allegiance. Baldwin I (known menacingly as Iron Arm), whose residence was a castle in the Burg in Bruges, is the first count of Flanders we know by name.

Wealthy citizens

During what became known as the 'Joyful Entry' into Bruges in 1301, Queen Joan I of Navarre marvelled at the rich apparel of the citizens: 'I thought I was the only queen, but there are hundreds more around me!'

Baldwin seems to have pursued a fierce expansionist policy to establish his rule over a large chunk of Flanders. In the 11th century, the succession passed to Robert the Frisian, who made Bruges his capital. Despite the ongoing power struggles, the cloth towns of Flanders flourished in the 12th and 13th centuries. Ghent became the largest town in Western Europe, while Bruges had a population as large as that of medieval London, trading with the Orient, the Middle East and the rest of Europe.

International banks made Bruges their headquarters, foreign embassies located there, and the first stock exchange in Europe was founded in the city. Wool was vital to the Flemish economy: Bruges, Ghent and Ypres (Ieper) all prospered from the export of their manufactured cloth, and depended on imported wool from England. Bruges dominated the trade in wool and, as a result, came to trade with the Hanseatic League, a powerful economic alliance of trading towns in northern Europe. The prosperity of the city reached a peak early in the 14th century.

However, tension grew between Bruges' merchants and its lords, the former tied to the English monarchy and its control over the supply of wool, the latter coerced by the hegemony of the French king. In the 13th and 14th centuries, the cloth towns of Flanders were scenes of frequent hostilities. The city walls of Bruges, the outline of which is preserved in the ring canal and its park, were built during the 14th century. Four of the nine original gates survive today, powerful bastions that give some idea of past defensive strength.

The most famous conflict became known as the 'Bruges Matins'. The French king, Philip the Fair, had invaded Flanders and appointed a governor whose taxation and suppression of the powerful guilds of Bruges were so severe that on the night of 17–18 May 1302 the city revolted, led by Pieter de Coninck and Jan Breydel. The resentful rebels killed everyone they believed to be French. In the same year the French were also defeated by the Flemish, at the Battle of the Golden Spurs near Kortrijk (Courtrai).

In 1384 the region became part of the Burgundian realm. Duke Philip the Good of Burgundy became count of Flanders in 1419 and ushered in a new kind of rule. He administered his possessions in Burgundy from Bruges, and was the patron of numerous artists, including Hans Memling; the court became renowned for its splendour. In 1429 Philip received his fiancée, Isabella of Portugal, in Bruges – the cause for a celebration of sumptuous ostentation.

Philip's successor, Charles the Bold, and his bride Margaret of York enjoyed a lavish wedding in Bruges when, it was said, the fountains spouted Burgundian wine. However, the splendour of Charles's reign did not last, and his death precipitated another French invasion of the south of the Low Countries. The people of Flanders took the opportunity to kidnap Charles's daughter Mary, forcing her

Rogier van der Weyden's portrait of Philip the Good

in a charter to renew their civic rights (curtailed by Philip) before they would help fight the French.

THE HABSBURGS

Maximilian of Austria married Mary and assumed full control of the region immediately after her death in 1482. The era of the powerful Habsburgs had begun. The burghers of Bruges still had the nerve to incarcerate Maximilian himself briefly in 1488, exacting further promises to acknowledge their rights, but Maximilian reneged on these as soon as he was released. His grandson Charles V, born in Ghent in 1500, continued a policy of favouring Antwerp rather than the cloth towns of Flanders, despite his reception in Bruges amid great pomp and ceremony in 1520. Charles' policy accelerated the economic decline of Bruges, which now had to contend with stiff competition from the cloth manufacturers in England. Bruges' economic death knell came when the River Zwin silted up, cutting off the town from the sea and ending its international trade; it did not awaken from its economic slumber until the 19th century.

THE REFORMATION

The Reformation was bound to have strong appeal for the merchants and weavers of Flanders. It stressed the rights of individuals

TRADE CENTRE

The city's early prosperity depended on its role as the chief port of Flanders, a hub for the English and Scandinavian trade. Right up until the 11th century, ships sailed right into the centre of town on the River Reie. Later, seagoing ships went as far as Damme, from where smaller vessels handled canal traffic with Bruges. It was one of the most important textile centres in northwest Europe.

to read and interpret the Word of God for themselves, thanks to the invention of the printing press, and questioned the clergy's power to promulgate a worldview controlled by an alliance of State and Church. With the emergence of Luther and Calvin, pressure for reform turned into outright revolt, leading to the establishment of alternative churches. Protestantism was born.

Charles the Bold of Burgundy

The Low Countries were particularly receptive to new ideas, as rich merchants chafed against the strictures of a rigidly hierarchical social system, while the artisanal guilds had always resented royal authority.

Charles V's abdication in 1556 passed the Low Countries to his very Catholic son, Philip II of Spain. Bloody conflict ensued. Philip and his sister Margaret harshly repressed Protestantism and tried to reinstate the authority of the Catholic Church. The 1565 harvest failure caused widespread famine and led to the Iconoclastic Fury, when workers ran riot among the Catholic churches, sacking and destroying everything. Frightened for their own positions, the nobility sided with Margaret and Philip. In 1567 Philip sent an army to the Low Countries. The 'Pacification of Ghent', signed in the city in 1576, instated a short-lived period of peace and freedom of worship.

A subsequent war between the Spanish and the Dutch Protestants, led by William the Silent, resulted in the Low Countries being partitioned in 1579, with the Protestant north ultimately gaining independence and the Catholic south retaining its Spanish Habsburg monarch. This partition corresponds more or less to today's border between Belgium and the Netherlands.

WAR OF THE SPANISH SUCCESSION

The Habsburg dynasty in Spain ended in 1700 when Charles II died without an heir. He had specified that Philip V of Anjou should succeed him, but the Habsburg Leopold II of Austria had other ideas. He did not like the thought of the grandson of the king of France ruling Spain, thus uniting the two kingdoms under one dynasty. He was prepared to fight for this conviction and the resulting war lasted from 1701 to 1714.

The treaty that ended the war signed over the Spanish Netherlands (now Belgium) to Austrian rule. They remained in

LITERARY REVIVAL

In literature, the 19th century saw something of a flourish in Flanders. Hendrik Conscience's 1838 novel *De Leeuw van Vlaanderen (The Lion of Flanders)* re-examined the revolt against the French in 1302, when a Flemish peasant army slaughtered the flower of French chivalry at the Battle of the Golden Spurs. Georges Rodenbach's 1892 novel *Bruges-la-Morte (Dead Bruges)* resonates with the air of mystery and decay into which Bruges had declined. Charles de Coster's *The Glorious Adventures of Tijl Uilenspiegel* (1867) provided neighbouring Damme with its legendary local hero. The Catholic priest Guido Gezelle breathed new life into Flemish poetry with his volumes *Kerkhofblommen (Graveyard Flowers,* 1858*), Tijdkrans (Time's Garland,* 1893) and *Rijmsnoer (String of Rhymes,* 1897), poems dealing with nature, religion and Flemish nationalism, in a mixture of literary Dutch and West Flanders dialect.

Bruges' history is told in murals in the Stadhuis (Town Hall)

Austrian hands under Archduchess Maria Theresa, and prospered through an arrangement whereby trade was subsidised by Austria.

In 1780, Maria Theresa was succeeded by her son Joseph II. He fancied himself as a radical ruler and did institute several enlightened, secularising reforms, but his lack of consultation and his 'top-down' approach to change created widespread resentment. Sporadic rebellions occurred from 1788, and in 1790 the 'United States of Belgium' was proclaimed, winning recognition from Britain and the Netherlands. The fledgling nation was defeated a year later by the forces of the new Austrian Emperor, Leopold II.

FRENCH INVASION AND INDEPENDENCE

Despite having received military assistance from a Belgian contingent against the Austrians in 1792, the army of revolutionary France invaded Belgium and the Netherlands two years later and occupied the annexed countries for the next 20 years – though not without some benefit to Belgium. The country was divided into a number of *départements* along French lines, while important and unjust aspects of Church, State, and taxation were reformed or abolished. There was also rapid industrialisation, with France being the main market for Belgian manufactured goods.

However, a majority of Belgians resented French occupation. Rebellions broke out from 1798 onwards. Following the final defeat of Napoleon at the Battle of Waterloo in 1815, the Congress of Vienna perpetuated Belgium's subjugation by passing control to the Dutch House of Orange in the person of William II, the king of the Netherlands. It was not until the revolution in 1830 that an independent and free Belgian state was created. In 1831, the London Conference recognised the independence of Belgium and established it as a constitutional monarchy. Leopold I, a German princeling, was awarded the crown.

ARMAGEDDON – TWICE

Throughout the 19th century, Belgium modernised, immersing itself in the Industrial Revolution. Slowly, Bruges was being rediscovered by British travellers on their way to the site of the Battle of Waterloo. Ghent revived, becoming a major economic centre. Yet tensions between different linguistic groups became more obvious as social difficulties failed to be resolved.

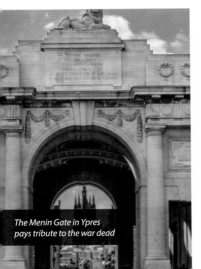

The Menin Gate in Ypres pays tribute to the war dead

In need of a scapegoat, the predominantly Dutch-speaking (and increasingly prosperous) north agitated for independence from the (French-speaking) Walloon south. Instead of attending to the problems of his country, the new king of Belgium, Leopold II (1865–1909) devoted most of his time to personal interests, including a private colony in the Belgian Congo. The colonial cruelties inflicted on the Congolese by Leopold and his agents were soon to become infamous right across Europe. In 1909 his nephew succeeded him, as Albert I.

> **Famine in Flanders**
>
> In the mid-19th century, living conditions for working people were appalling, aggravated by a dreadful famine in Flanders from 1845 to 1848. Almost half the population of Bruges was dependent on charity.

During Albert's reign, World War I gripped Belgium for four years. In 1914, the German army invaded, despite the country's neutrality, forcing the king to move to a narrow remaining strip of unoccupied Belgium. His resistance to the invaders gained him international renown and much domestic popularity as the 'Soldier King'.

The war's northern front extended roughly diagonally across the country, with the most infamous, and bloodiest, of battles taking place around Ypres (Ieper) in western Flanders. The defeat of Germany won Belgium considerable reparations and some new territory.

It might have been expected that the experience of war would draw the nation together, especially when King Albert proclaimed a series of reforms meant to improve equality between the Flemish and the Walloons. However, fascism was already working its way through the north and the communities grew more antagonistic. In 1940, the German army marched into Belgium, occupying it in just three weeks. Bruges suffered little damage, though its new canal had to be repaired extensively.

A resistance movement formed, including an underground network to protect Belgium's Jews. However, the behaviour of the king, Leopold III, who was eager to accommodate the invaders, caused much controversy after the war as Belgium sought to rebuild itself. In 1950, the people voted by a narrow margin to ask the king home from exile, but Leopold decided to abdicate in favour of his son, Baudouin I.

REGIONALISATION

After forming Benelux, an economic union with the Netherlands and Luxembourg, Belgium went on to join the European Economic Community in 1957, with Brussels the seat of the organisation. Though this has ensured that Belgium is internationally recognised as the home of European bureaucracy, it has nevertheless retained its own distinct national character.

The country finally divested itself of the Congo (now the Democratic Republic of Congo) in 1960. Internal political events since the end of World War II have been dominated by continuing friction between the Flemish and Walloons. In 1977, three federal regions were established – Wallonia, Flanders and Brussels – in an attempt to ease the tensions between the groups by giving them greater self-determination. In 1989, regional governments were created, each with responsibility for all policy except matters concerning social security, defence and foreign affairs. A new constitution was adopted in 1994, establishing Belgium as a federal state.

In practice, visitors will see little sign of intercommunity tension and the unifying presence of King Philippe and the royal family helps to preserve a sense of nationhood. Bruges' ambitious restoration of its medieval centre continues to attract tourists from all over the world. But it refuses to be pigeon-holed as a dead, medieval town, and looks instead to the future.

HISTORICAL LANDMARKS

58–50 BC Roman conquest of Gaul, including present-day Belgium.

AD498 Conversion to Christianity of Frankish King Clovis.

768 Charlemagne's unified Frankish kingdom is established.

Early 800s Castle (Burg) built at Bruges.

851 First certain mention of Bruges.

864 Baldwin becomes first known Count of Flanders.

11th century Silting of the River Zwin helps cut off Bruges's access to the sea.

1150 Count Thierry returns from Crusades with Relic of the Holy Blood.

1302 Bruges Matins and Battle of the Golden Spurs.

1384 Flanders becomes part of Burgundian kingdom.

1419 Philip the Good of Burgundy becomes count of Flanders.

1482 Habsburg reign begins with Maximilian of Austria.

1556 Charles V abdicates; Philip II of Spain succeeds.

1567–79 Religious wars in the southern Low Countries.

1790 Proclamation – albeit short-lived - of United States of Belgium.

1794 French invade and occupy country for 20 years.

1815 Napoleon defeated at Waterloo; Congress of Vienna.

1830 Belgian revolution and independence.

1914–18 World War I; Germans invade neutral Belgium.

1940 Nazi Germany occupies Belgium during World War II.

1977 Establishment of Flanders as one of three federal Belgian regions.

1993 Albert II becomes king of the Belgians.

2002 The Concertgebouw concert and opera hall opens in the city.

2008 Bruges is the setting for the hit black-comedy film *In Bruges*.

2013 King Philippe assumes the throne after the abdication of his father Albert II. Socialist Renaat Landuyt becomes Bruges' mayor.

2016 35 people are killed in three coordinated suicide attacks carried out by the so-called Islamic State in Brussels.

2022 King Phillippe visits the Congo and regrets his country's colonial record – but doesn't offer reparations.

2024 After a major electoral defeat, Alexander De Croo resigned but remains as caretaker prime minister until a new government is formed.

A canal trip in Bruges

OUT AND ABOUT

Bruges is made for walking: it is very compact, with attractions clearly signposted. It has been dubbed the 'Venice of the North', and while this comparison is unfair to both places, it should come as no surprise that canal cruises are one of the best ways of viewing the city: central Bruges has 10km (6 miles) of canals, and 4km (2.5 miles) of them are accessible by boat tour.

The capital of West Flanders, Bruges is Belgium's most popular tourist destination, so be prepared for large crowds in the summer. This doesn't diminish the city's charm, but it does mean queues for the main sights and art galleries may be longer, so try to plan in advance. Many visitors arrive for the day by bus, so if you're staying overnight you can wander in peace come evening. Ambling through the city's narrow streets and open marketplaces is a pleasure, with charming views around each and every corner – there is always something else to delight the eye and fire up the imagination.

It was Bruges' five centuries of economic decline that preserved the buildings we now enjoy; there was never any money to demolish and rebuild. The badly dilapidated city was 'discovered' by visitors in the 19th century. In the quieter residential quarters you can still sense what it must have been like to walk through the streets of a forgotten town, your footsteps

Bruges Museum Pass

If you plan on visiting several of the city's museums, it may be worth buying the **Museum Card** (www.museabrugge.be/en). Valid for three consecutive days, it costs €33 (there are youth discounts) and grants free entry to 13 municipal museums.

The Belfort (belfry)

ringing on the cobble-stones, while church bells chime and a horse's hooves echo from a nearby street.

One of the first things to strike visitors is the harmonious appearance of the architecture. The characteristic stepped gables of the houses may be a bit worn with age, but this only adds to their charm. You will notice that most buildings are of brick, with their shutters and woodwork painted in traditional Bruges red. Bruges is now so beautifully restored that you may briefly find yourself yearning for something less perfect just by way of contrast; Belgians themselves describe the place as an outdoor museum.

Enjoy the route suggested here, but also take the time to improvise and discover the city on your own, perhaps simply following the canals, or tracing the path of the city walls with their big, imposing gates. Horse-drawn carriages and bicycle taxis can also be hired.

Our walk begins at the **Markt** ❶, Bruges' main square. Before you set off, make sure to take time to look around. This may be the 21st century, but not much has changed since some of the civic buildings and houses that you can see were constructed; it's not hard to imagine what the place would have looked like in the city's bustling golden age, when merchants flocked here from all over Europe.

SOUTH FROM THE MARKT

On the southeast side of the square, dominating the skyline, is the magnificent **Belfort** (belfry; www.museabrugge.be/en). One of the first priorities of any visitor is to ignore the 1m (3ft) lean of the 83m (272ft) belfry and climb its 366 steps for a breath-taking view of the town and surrounding countryside. The best times to climb it are early morning or late afternoon. The belfry dates from the 13th century, when Bruges was at the height of its prosperity, but the final storey (with the clock) is 15th-century. The second floor houses a treasury where the town seal and charters were kept safely behind intricate Romanesque grilles (built in 1292), each requiring nine separate keys to open them.

You may already have heard the 47-bell carillon, which weighs 27 tons and hangs in the tower above. The belfry is an excellent landmark when you're finding your way around. The Belfort is attached to the **Hallen**, a rectangular courtyard, also dating from the 13th century, which would once have been crammed with traders, the air heavy with the scent of spices brought by Venetian merchants. A canal lay below the covered market, which was used for the loading and unloading of goods, but this was filled uin many centuries ago.

The neo-Gothic **Provinciaal Hof**, located on the east side of the Markt, once housed the West Flanders provincial government (not open to visitors) and beside it is the **Historium** (www.historium.be), a garish and gaudy interactive museum depicting life in the Middle Ages.

Bruges Matins

At the centre of the Markt is a 19th-century monument to the heroes of the Bruges Matins (see page 15), Pieter De Coninck and Jan Breydel. Stained green with age, they still look suitably determined.

The **Craenenburg**, on the opposite side of the square, now an atmospheric café-brasserie, was where the Habsburg Crown Prince Maximilian of Austria was briefly imprisoned in 1488. The future emperor, understandably disgruntled, did his best ever afterwards to promote trade through Antwerp at the expense of Bruges (see page 16).

On the same side of the square, at the corner of Sint-Amandsstraat, is a beautiful 15th-century brick building, **Huis Bouchoute**. Restored in 1995 to its original brick, including removing later rooftop crenulations, this house hosted the exiled English King Charles II in 1656–7. The roof-mounted octagonal compass and weathervane (1682) allowed Bruges' merchants to judge their ships' chances of entering or leaving the port.

THE BURG

A stroll down Breidelstraat, in the southeast corner of the Markt (next to the Hallen), takes you past narrow De Garre, the shortest street in Bruges; if you need refreshment, there's a cosy 100-beer bar at the end, the Staminee de Garre. Breidelstraat lsoon eads to the **Burg ❷**, one of Europe's finest medieval squares, named after the castle built here by the Count of Flanders, the bellicose Baldwin Iron Arm.

Which building in the square is the most splendid? It's a hard choice. On the corner of Breidelstraat and the Burg is the ornate Baroque **Proosdij** (Provost's House), formerly the palace of the bishops of Bruges, dating from 1666. Its parapet is lined with urns and topped with a handsome female personification of justice armed with sword and scales. The building stands near the site of the demolished Sint-Donaaskerk (St Donatian's), a Carolingian-style church built around 950.

The **Stadhuis** (Town Hall; www.visitbruges.be) on the south side of the Burg was constructed between 1376 and 1420. It is one of the oldest town halls in Belgium and a Gothic masterpiece, its delicately traced windows framed within pilasters topped with octagonal turrets. If you stand close to the building its statues and spiral chimneys seem to be curving down over you, and the detailing of the sandstone facade becomes even more impressive. The statues on the facade are of the counts and countesses of Flanders.

The splendid Stadhuis is a Gothic masterpiece

The exterior of the Stadhuis promises great things and the interior of the magnificent town hall will certainly not let you down. Bluestone stairs lead from the flag-draped entrance hall to the first-floor Gothic Hall, a splendid room that witnessed the first meeting of the States General, set up in 1464 by the dukes of Burgundy to regulate provincial contributions to the treasury. The vaulted oak ceiling, with its long pendant keystones at the junctions of the arches, is richly decorated in tones of brown, black, maroon and gold, surrounding painted scenes from the New Testament.

The murals depict important events in the city's history. The De Vriendt brothers painted them in 1905 after the original medieval wall decorations were lost. The small, delicate balcony near the entrance door was for the town pipers and other musicians. The hall is used for civic ceremonies, receptions and weddings. An adjoining room – the **Historische zaal** (History Room) – features an intriguing audio-visual display exploring the city's relationship with the sea and the interminable cycle of dredging and embankment that this has entailed.

To the right of the Stadhuis as you face it is the small, gilded entrance to the **Basiliek van het Heilig-Bloed** (Basilica of the Holy Blood; www.holyblood.com). Its three-arched facade was completed by 1534, making it a mere youth in comparison with the Stadhuis. Its ornate stone carvings and statues of angels, knights and their ladies stand below two adjoining towers of great delicacy. The interior of the basilica is divided into two chapels, a 12th-century Romanesque lower chapel and a Gothic upper chapel, providing a dramatic contrast in styles. The lower chapel is a study in shadows, with austere, unadorned lines, uncompromising Romanesque pillars, and little decoration except for a relief carving over an interior doorway depicting the baptism of St Basil (an early Church Father). St Basil's relics were brought back from Palestine by Robert II, count of Flanders. The faded carving is childlike in style, its naivety emphasised by the two mismatched columns supporting it.

Ascension Day

On Ascension Day every year, the holy relic is carried through Bruges in the famous Heilig-Bloed Processie (Procession of the Holy Blood), the most important of West Flanders' religious festivals. The venerated phial is transported in a flamboyant gold and silver reliquary that is normally kept in the treasury off the chapel.

Access to the upper chapel is through a beautiful late-Gothic doorway. Ascending by a broad, elegant 16th-century spiral staircase, you can enter the upper chapel beneath the organ case. The lines of the chapel have been spoiled somewhat by over-enthusiastic 19th-century decoration and murals, but the greater impression is of warmth and richness. The ceiling looks like an upturned boat and the room is flooded with a golden light. The bronze-coloured pulpit is a curious sight, bearing a remarkable resemblance to a cored and stuffed tomato.

The Basilica of the Holy Blood

In a small side chapel you will find the holy relic from which the church derives its name. Flemish knight Dirk of Alsace returned from the Second Crusade in the Holy Land in 1149 and is said to have brought with him a crystal phial believed to contain some drops of Christ's blood. Once venerated all over medieval Europe, it is still brought out each Friday for the faithful. The dried blood turned to liquid at regular intervals for many years, an event declared by Pope Clement V to be a miracle. The phial is stored in a richly ornate silver tabernacle presented by the Habsburg archdukes of Spain in 1611. It is carried in procession through the streets every year on Ascension Day.

Footsteps from the basilica, beyond the Stadhuis, the **Landhuis van het Brugse Vrije** (Liberty of Bruges Palace) is an early 18th-century neoclassical building on the site of an older structure that used to house the law courts: at the rear of the building overlooking the canal are the remains of an attractive 16th-century facade.

Part of the palatial building now houses the **Brugse Vrije** (Liberty of Bruges; www.museabrugge.be/en), with an entrance at Burg 11. The museum has one main exhibit, the **Renaissancezaal** (Renaissance Hall), the Liberty's restored council chamber. The great black marble and oak Renaissance 'Emperor Charles' chimneypiece, designed by the painter Lanceloot Blondeel in tribute to Charles V, was started in 1528 and finished in 1531. This is one of the most memorable artworks in Bruges: the carving is on a monumental scale, covering an entire wall and joining the ceiling with carved tendrils and caskets. A statue of Charles in full armour, wearing the emblem of the Order of the Golden Fleece, is in the centre. Forty-six coats of arms and ribbons of wood also appear on it. Among many of the scenes, the design depicts the defeat of the French at Pavia and the biblical story of Susanna and the Elders. The intricate craftsmanship of the piece is superb and quite overwhelming, but the handholds for gentlemen to use while drying their boots are the sort of domestic touch everyone remembers.

Adjoining this building is the statue-laden, Renaissance-style façade of the **Oude Civiele Griffie** (Old Registrar's House), completed in 1537. Note how the sinuously curved and scrolled gables contrast with the older, linear step gables of most of the architecture in Bruges.

AROUND VISMARKT

Wander through the Renaissance arch joining the Oude Civiele Griffie and the Stadhuis, and follow Blinde Ezelstraat (Blind Donkey Street) across the bridge until you reach the colonnaded **Vismarkt** ❸ (Fishmarket; open access). Built in 1821, the market sells fresh fish from the North Sea along with a variety of craft items. Lining both sides of the canal are some pretty little streets.

At Groenerei (left at the bridge) is the 1634 **Godshuis De Pelikaanhuis** (Pelican House). Easily identified by its pelican emblem over the doorway, this was once a hospital, or almshouse. Such almshouses can be found all over Bruges: the city's guilds and wealthy merchants built them to shelter the sick, elderly and poor. They are usually low, whitewashed cottages like the ones in Zwarteleertouwerstraat (take the last right turn in Groenerei).

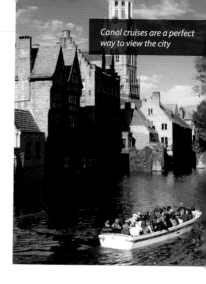

Canal cruises are a perfect way to view the city

Back behind the Vismarkt, you can wander through Huidenvettersplein (Tanners' Square), which has become something of a tourist hotspot crowded with cafés and restaurants. Thus, the turreted **Huidevettershuis** (Tanners' Guild Hall), built in 1630, is now a restaurant.

Beyond the square, **Rozenhoedkaai** (Rosary Quay) is one of the places from where boat tours depart; do stop to enjoy the view from the quay. The Dijver, a canalised branch of the Reie, begins at **Sint-Jan Nepomucenusbrug** (St John of Nepomuk Bridge). A statue portrays the good man himself, appropriately the patron saint of bridges. The tree-lined riverbank is the site of a weekend antiques market; the river passes superb old houses and crosses the canal into Gruuthusestraat. On the left are a pair of museums: the Groeninge and the Gruuthuse.

THE GROENINGE MUSEUM

The **Groeninge Museum** ❹ (www.museabrugge.be/en) contains some of the great works of the Flemish Primitives, including Van Eyck's portrait of his wife Margareta, which is so typical of the painter's incredible realism; and Bosch's deeply disturbing

Last Judgement, with the fires of hell ablaze. The *Judgement of Cambyses*, painted by Gerard David in 1498, depicts the judicial skinning of a corrupt judge while detached onlookers coolly observe the proceedings.

Other treasures include Memling's glorious *Moreel Triptych* depicting St Christopher with portraits in the side panels, and his *St John Altarpiece*. In addition, there are magnificent portraits by Hugo van der Goes, Rogier van der Weyden and Petrus Christus, as well as paintings by unknown masters, many of them depicting detailed views of the city.

However, the greatest work in the museum is Van Eyck's *Madonna and Child with Canon Joris van der Paele*, where the textures and folds of the clothing and carpets are reproduced with breath-taking effect. There is also work from later periods,

'Madonna and Child' by Jan Van Eyck, 1436

including a landscape by James Ensor, enigmatic work by René Magritte, and some pieces by Flemish Expressionists – but the early Flemish artists steal the show.

Inland lighthouse

The 122m (400ft) brick tower of Onze-Lieve-Vrouwekerk (the second highest in Belgium) once served as a kind of inland lighthouse for ships on their way to Bruges.

THE GRUUTHUSE MUSEUM

Footsteps from the Groeninge Museum, the **Gruuthusemuseum** ❺ (www.visitbruges.be) occupies a rambling mansion that dates back to the fifteenth-century. The mansion takes its name from the house owners' historical right to tax the *gruut* used by brewers as it arrived in the city – the gruut being the herbs, spices and plants used in brewing before the introduction of hops. The Gruuthuse has twice sheltered fugitive English kings – both Edward IV and Charles II stayed here – and today it holds a wide-ranging collection of Flemish fine, applied and decorative art. Its strongest suit is its superb collection of tapestries, mostly woven in Brussels or Bruges in the sixteenth and seventeenth centuries.

ONZE-LIEVE-VROUWEKERK

The exterior of **Onze-Lieve-Vrouwekerk** ❻ (Church of Our Lady; www.museabrugge.be) is a mix of different styles and is slightly forbidding. More interesting is the interior, which is dotted with religious artworks and treasures. Chief among them is the *Madonna and Child* (1504) by Michelangelo, originally intended for Siena Cathedral and the only one of his works to travel outside Italy during his lifetime. It was brought to Bruges by a Flemish merchant called Jan van Moeskroen. The Madonna is a subdued, preoccupied figure, while the infant leans nonchalantly on her knee.

Michelangelo's Madonna and Child in Onze-Lieve-Vrouwekerk

There are some fine paintings here by Pieter Pourbus (*Last Supper* and *Adoration of the Shepherds*) and Gerard David (*Transfiguration*), but, after the Michelangelo, it is the chancel area that holds most interest. Here you can see the **tombs** of Charles the Bold and his daughter Mary of Burgundy, fine examples of Renaissance carving. Both are richly decorated with coats of arms linked with floral motifs in copper-gilt gold, reds and blues. The figures themselves, which have domestic details like the pet dogs at Mary's feet, are also in copper gilt. Whether or not Charles and Mary are actually buried here is a matter of some dispute. Charles was killed in battle in Nancy in 1477 and it was difficult to identify the body afterwards. Mary (who died in a riding accident at the age of 25, bringing to a close the 100-year reign of the House of Burgundy) may be buried among a group of poly-chromed tombs that were unearthed beneath the tombs in 1979. You can see the frescoed tombs through windows in the floor and mirrors in front of the sarcophagi.

Elsewhere in the church, you will find the funerary chapel of Pieter Lanchals (see page 38), containing frescoed tombs in maroon and black; and Van Dyck's starkly atmospheric painting of Christ on the Cross. The splendid wooden gallery overlooking the chancel belongs to the adjacent Gruuthuse mansion (see page 35) and dates from the 15th century.

SINT-JANSHOSPITAALMUSEUM

Opposite the church is **Sint-Janshospitaalmuseum** ❼ (St John's Hospital Museum; www.museabrugge.be). Constructed in the 12th century, this is one of the oldest buildings in Bruges. The hospital was still functioning in the 19th century, and today a series of interesting displays explores the medical care and attention offered here. Included is an exhibition of historical documents and alarming surgical instruments.

The old hospital's main event, exhibited in the former chapel, are seven masterpieces by the Flemish master Hans Memling. Each of the exhibited works displays Memling's captivating attention to detail and mastery of realism. It is impossible to pick the 'best', but probably the most famous is the detailed *Reliquary of St Ursula*, one of the greatest art treasures in the country. Commissioned by two sisters who worked in the church, the reliquary is in the form of a miniature Gothic chapel with Memling's painted panels in the positions of the windows.

The *Mystic Marriage of St Catherine* includes St John the Evangelist and St John the Baptist, patron saints of the hospital: it has been suggested that saints Catherine and Barbara are portraits of Mary of Burgundy and Margaret of York. A painting by Jan Beerbloch depicts the relaxed standards of

The canal frontage of Sint-Janshospitaalmuseum

hospital hygiene: nurses sweep the floors while dogs wander the wards.

AROUND MARIASTRAAT

If you head south along Mariastraat and look left along Nieuwe Gentweg, there are some typical almshouses that have gardens open to the public. The next turning on the right is Walstraat, a peaceful street of delightful 16th- and 17th-century gabled houses where lacemaking is still practised (outside on warm days).

If your thirst for culture is overtaken by a thirst for something else, a short stroll will bring you to **Brouwerij De Halve Maan** (The Half Moon; www.halvemaan.be; guided tours) at Walplein 26. Belgium is well known for its many hundreds of beers, and Bruges beers are exceptionally good. De Halve Maan has been brewing in the city since 1564 and today produces a light, highly fermented local beer called Straffe Hendrik (Strong Henry, after its high-alcohol content). Brugse Zot beer joined it in 2005. The 45-minute tour of the museum will reveal how it is done, and includes an ascent to the roof for a good view over the gables of central Bruges. The building is suffused with a sweet smell from the brewing process. At the end of the visit, each visitor gets a drink in the congenial bar, lined with every conceivable shape of beer bottle.

Why the swans?

There have been swans on Minnewater, so the story goes, since 1488 when Emperor Maximilian was imprisoned in Bruges and his councillor, Pieter Lanchals, was beheaded. Lanchals' coat of arms featured a swan, and the emperor ordered that swans be kept on the canals of Bruges for evermore, as a reminder of the city's dreadful crime.

THE BEGIJNHOF

South of the church along Mariastraat, follow the

signposts to the **Begijnhof** . Belgium is famous for its many residences for religious orders, its *begijnhofs* constructed for unmarried or widowed women (known as Beguines). These women lived under religious rule without having to commit themselves to the full vows of a nun. The women cared for the sick and made a living by lacemaking. Items varied from doilies to dresses.

The Begijnhof

The **Prinselijk Begijnhof ten Wijngaarde** (Princely Beguinage of the Vineyard; daily 6.30am–6.30pm; free) was founded in 1245 by Margaret of Constantinople and remained a Beguine residence until its conversion into a Benedictine convent in the 20th century. The convent is one of the most attractive Beguine residences in the country. Reached by a bridge over the canal and through an arch, it comprises a circle of white, 17th-century houses set around a courtyard of grass and trees that comes alive with daffodils each spring. In a city replete with picturesque views, this is one of the most photographed places. You can visit the Begijnhof's church, **Onze-Lieve-Vrouw van Troost van Spermalie** (Our Lady of Consolation of Spermalie), when the nuns are having a service. A stroll around the tree-shaded cloister garden, a blaze of colour in spring and summer, is a delight.

Around the Begijnhof the street layout is as it was in the 17th century, so take time to wander around and enjoy the views. This

is also where the hard-working carriage horses of Bruges stop to enjoy a well-earned rest mid-tour, with a drink of water pumped from a horse's head statue.

MINNEWATER

The picturesque and understandably popular park and lake of **Minnewater** ❾ (Lake of Love) lie to the south of Walplein and Wijngaardplein. The lake was originally the inner harbour of Bruges, before the Zwin inlet silted up and cut off the city from the sea; you can still see the 15th-century Sashuis (Lock House). Beyond the Sashuis, the tower on the right is the **Poertoren** (Powder Tower), a remnant of old fortifications. On the east side of the basin is leafy **Minnewater Park**, in which stands **Kasteel Minnewater** (Minnewater Castle).

Take Wijngaardstraat and turn right into Noordstraat, to the **Godshuis de Vos** (1713). You can look over the wall into the courtyard of this enchanting almshouse, where the original eight little houses are now converted to six.

KATELIJNESTRAAT

Turn left into Arsenalstraat and left again into busy Katelijnestraat, where, at No. 43, you'll find the **Diamantmuseum** ❿ (Diamond Museum; www.diamondmuseum.be). The museum documents the history of diamond polishing, a technique thought to have been invented by the Bruges goldsmith Lodewijk van Berquem in the mid-15th century. There is a reconstruction of van Berquem's workshop, some examples of tools and machinery used in diamond polishing, plus models, paintings and rare rock samples. Demonstrations further illustrate the technique.

Katalijnestraat connects with Nieuwe Gentweg, where you can visit a cluster of attractive *godshuizen* (almshouses): **De Meulenaere** (dating from 1613); **Sint-Jozef** (St Joseph; 1674); and, around the corner in Drie Kroezenstraat, **Onze-Lieve-Vrouw van de Zeven Weeën** (Our Lady of the Seven Sorrows, founded in 1654).

WEST FROM THE MARKT

Go along Steenstraat, a beautiful street lined with gabled guild houses, headquarters of the trading and craft guilds that contributed so much to the medieval city's life. There is the Bakers' Guild House at No. 19, the Stonemasons' Guild House at No. 25, the Joiners' Guild House at No. 38,

Zandfeesten

On a Saturday morning 't Zand Square hosts one of Belgium's biggest street markets. The vast Zandfeesten (Zand Festival; www.brugsezandfeesten.be) flea market is also held here a few times each year.

and the Shoemakers' Guild House at No. 40. All of these now house either shops or banks. This brings you to **Simon Stevinplein**, and its bronze sculpture of the Bruges mathematician and scientist Simon Stevin, who fled from his native city around 1580 during the anti-Protestant persecutions carried out by its Hapsburg rulers. He later lived and worked in Holland. The square was laid out in 1819 and the statue, which depicts Stevin holding a set of dividers in one hand and a manuscript in the other, dates from 1847.

If you make a short detour south of Simon Stevinplein to Oude Burg, you will find the **Hof van Watervliet**. The 16th-century buildings have been much restored, but are still of interest. Former residents included the humanist scholar Erasmus and the exiled Charles II of England.

Further along Steenstraat you will come to **Sint-Salvatorskathedraal** ⓫ (Saint Saviour's Cathedral; www.sintsalvatorskathedraal.be; free; worshippers only during services). The oldest parish church in Bruges, it has been a cathedral since 1834, replacing the city centre cathedral destroyed by an invading French army in the late 18th century. Parts of the building date from the 12th and 13th centuries, though the church was originally founded in the 10th century. The Gothic interior is quite Spartan and curiously unfocused in design, but the choir stalls and the Baroque rood screen showing God the Father are worth a look. The cathedral treasury, is located off the right transept. Specialising in liturgical objects, it is worth visiting for its Flemish paintings, including work by Dirk Bouts and Pieter Pourbus.

AROUND 'T ZAND SQUARE

Continuing along Zuidzandstraat, you come to bustling **'t Zand** ⓬, a square lined with numerous hotels and cafés. Notice the fountain and groups of modern sculpture by Stefaan Depuydt and Livia Canestraro. The four female figures in *Bathing Women* symbolise

The Cyclists, in 't Zand Square

Antwerp, Bruges, Kortrijk and Ghent; *Landscape of Flanders* is an abstract representation of the region's flat terrain; *The Cyclists* is an expression of youth and hope for the future; and *The Fishermen* represents Bruges' ancient ties with the sea.

Along Boeveriestraat from 't Zand, at Klokstraat, is the **Kapucijnenkerk** (Capuchin Church), the church of a Capuchin monastery built here in 1869 to replace an earlier one in what is now 't Zand Square. The monastery was demolished to make way for the city's original railway station, which has itself vanished. On the left side of Boeveriestraat stands the Benedictine **Sint-Godelieve Abdij** (St Godelina Abbey). The nuns first moved into the city in the 16th century and established themselves here in 1623. Behind its brick facade is a wide green lawn. Across the street, you will find the grounded **Dumery-Klok** (Dumery Bell). This used to hang in the belfry above the Markt and was placed here as a memento of the 18th-century Dumery Bell Foundry that once stood here. Also on this street and around the neighbourhood are the *godshuizen* (almshouses) **Van Campen** (1436), **Van Peenen** (1621), **Gloribus** (1634), **Sucx** (1436), and **De Moor** (1480).

The park that now occupies the line of the city's medieval wall and moat leads north, past the **Oud Waterhuis** (Old Water House; 1394), part of the city's water distribution system, which drew supplies from the canals and other sources. Continuing north brings you to the **Smedenpoort** (Marshal's Gate), one of the four fortified city gates that survive of the nine that were once dotted around the now mostly vanished city walls. Dating from 1368 with additions from the 17th century, it is a powerful-looking piece of military engineering.

Take Smedenstraat back towards 't Zand and the Markt. A short diversion into Kreupelenstraat lets you visit the **Onze-Lieve-Vrouw-van-Blindekenskapel** (Chapel of Our Lady of the Blind; daily 9am–5pm). This bright and simple 17th-century church has a carved pulpit from 1659 and a gilded 14th-century statue of the *Madonna and Child* above a side altar. Every 15 August, on the feast of the Assumption, a procession leaves from here and wends its way to the church of Onze-Lieve-Vrouw van de Potterie (Our Lady of the Pottery) in the northeast of the city (see page 53). A further diversion, this time along the handsome Speelmansrei canal, leads to the little Gothic

Golden Fleece

Philip the Good founded the chivalric Order of the Golden Fleece in 1430, on the occasion of his wedding to Isabella of Portugal. Its knights were the cream of Burgundian high society, but according to a scurrilous French report published in 1620, the Golden Fleece referred not to the mythological quest of Jason and the Argonauts, but to the lustrous hair of one of Philip's mistresses.

The Prinsenhof

Speelmanskapel (Minstrels' Church; 1421). The nearby **Stadspark Sebrechts** stands on land once occupied by the nuns of the Sint-Elisabethklooster, which was dissolved in 1784. In summer the park becomes an open-air museum of modern sculpture.

Nearby Noordzandstraat is the site of the **Prinsenhof** ⑬ (Prince's Court), once the residence of dukes and duchesses of Burgundy, and later of Habsburg emperors and empresses. During the Burgundian period it was the ultimate in pomp and splendour. When Charles the Bold was engaged in his ill-starred quest to make Burgundy a third continental power, alongside France and Germany, the Prinsenhof was a radiant nucleus, and Bruges the largest, richest and most powerful city north of the Alps. Burgundian-era highlights took place in this setting. Philip the Good celebrated his marriage to Isabella of Portugal in 1430 and Charles the Bold his marriage to Margaret of York in 1468, with banquets that made the term 'Burgundian' a byword for lavishness.

Duchess Mary gave birth to Philip the Handsome here in 1479, and in 1482 she died here, as had Philip the Good in 1467.

Not much survives of the 14th-century palace, yet the Prinsenhof is still imposing. Constantly remodelled throughout the Burgundian century, the palace was put up for sale in 1631 and purchased in 1662 by the Order of St Francis, for a convent. In 1794, the nuns departed for Delft, ahead of the incoming French Revolutionary army, and the property was sold again. In 1888, another group of nuns took possession, this time the French Dames de la Retraite. A century later the palace was sold to a private concern and used as a centre for exhibitions, conferences and concerts. It now houses the Hotel Dukes' Palace.

In little Muntplein square is a small equestrian statue, *Flandria Nostra*, of Mary of Burgundy riding side-saddle. The daughter of Charles the Bold, she died in 1482 at the age of 25, after falling from her horse while hunting. She now occupies a sarcophagus in the Church of Our Lady (see page 35). From here, it's a short stroll back to the Markt.

NORTH FROM THE MARKT

The city north of the Markt used to be the home and business premises of the merchants of medieval Bruges, for it was common practice to live and work in the same building. The avenues of elegant houses from this period are punctuated with grandiose mansions dating from the 18th century, and the canals here meet and diverge in broad highways of water. It is no wonder that many visitors regard this as their favourite part of the city.

JAN VAN EYCKPLEIN

Just a few minutes' walk north from the Markt along Vlamingstraat is **Jan van Eyckplein** ⓮ and adjoining Spiegelrei. Bruges has many former harbours, and this one was the busiest of them all; the canal that terminates here once extended as far as the Markt. It was also the commercial and diplomatic centre for medieval Bruges, and foreign consulates opened along the length of Spiegelrei.

The Poortersloge

There is a statue of the painter in the square, but it is the buildings that really stand out. Jan looks directly at the most striking of these, the **Poortersloge** (Burghers' Lodge; 1417). The pencil tower may point heavenwards, but the building was in fact the meeting place of the wealthier city merchants. On its facade is a statue of the bear that features in the city's coat of arms. It was also the emblem of a jousting club that held its events in the marketplace outside. The restored building now houses the Bruges State Archives.

To the right of the Poortersloge is the 15th-century **Tolhuis** (Customs House), where various owners levied tolls over the years, including the dukes of Luxembourg whose coat of arms is on the facade.

Adjacent Spanjaardstraat was the centre of the city's Spanish mercantile community in the 16th century and the many mansions in this area testify to their wealth. Among the best, at No. 16, is **Huis De la Torre** (c.1500), with an ornately decorated Gothic facade and a mid-16th-century Renaissance portal. Ignatius de Loyola, the Spanish priest who founded the Jesuit Order, was a

Jeruzalemkerk

frequent guest in the house at No. 9.

EAST OF JAN VAN EYCKPLEIN

From Jan van Eyckplein you can wander through the lovely canalside street of Spinolarei into Koningstraat and Sint-Maartensplein, where you will find **Sint-Walburgakerk** (Church of St Walpurga). Pieter Huyssens, the Bruges Jesuit and architect, built this impressive Baroque church in 1643. A statue of St Francis Xavier stands above the entrance door. The Baroque interior is for the most part unremarkable, except for the fabulous pulpit by Artus Quellin the Younger, which has a scalloped canopy uplifted by trumpeting angels.

Crossing the canal and following Sint-Annarei south into Sint-Annakerkstraat, you will see the slender spire of **Sint-Annakerk** (Church of St Anne), a 1624 Baroque replacement for the Gothic church demolished in 1561. Inside, the carving of the rood screen, confessionals and pulpit, as well as the rich panelling, are well worth viewing if the church is open.

The unusual tower with the vaguely Oriental look visible from Sint-Annakerk belongs to the **Jeruzalemkapel** ⓑ (Jerusalem Chapel; www.adornes.org), at Peperstraat 1. The church is modelled on the Church of the Holy Sepulchre in Jerusalem. Dating from 1428, it was built by the Adornes family, originally merchants from Genoa, who had travelled on a pilgrimage to Jerusalem. They were so impressed by the church that they built this one in Bruges. There is even a copy of Christ's memorial tomb in the crypt.

It is a sombre, stark place with good examples of 15th- and 16th-century stained glass, some of which depicts members of the Adornes family. In the nave you can see effigies of Anselmus Adornes and his wife. The altar is carved in a rather macabre fashion, with skulls and bones, and the cave-like atmosphere of the church is emphasised by the space behind the altar and above the crypt, which rises almost to the full height of the tower to create an eerie, artificial-looking cavern.

Close to the Jeruzalemkerk, at Balstraat 16, is the **Kantcentrum** (Lace Centre; www.kantcentrum.eu; see previous page), a splendid

LACEMAKING

Bruges' handmade lace is making a slow but sure comeback, thanks mainly to the demand from visiting tourists. At its peak in the 1840s, lacemaking provided steady employment – and low wages – for 10,000 local women and girls. Even in its heyday, lacemaking was a cottage industry. Handmade lace is expensive, and the majority of the items sold in the city's multitude of lace shops are machine-made and often imported.

The most popular kind of lace made in Bruges is bobbin lace, which is created using a technique developed in Flanders in the 16th century. Threads of silk, linen or cotton on as many as 700 different bobbins are crossed and braided around a framework of pins. It takes great skill and concentration to do this and it is fascinating to watch an experienced craftswoman (it generally is a woman) at work. Other styles of handmade Belgian lace are *bloemenwerk* (flower lace), *rozenkant* (pearled rosary) and *toveressesteek* (fairy stitch).

museum and workshop in the 15th-century Jeruzalem-godshuizen (almshouses) founded by the Adornes family. Here you can see fine examples of the craft of lacemaking and demonstrations by workers and their students.

Further down Balstraat from the Kantcentrum is the **Volkskundemuseum** (Folklore Museum; www.visitbrugge.be), housed in a delightful row of 17th-century whitewashed almshouses built by the cobblers' guild. The life of everyday West Flanders is recreated in the traditionally furnished interiors, including a primary school class, coopers' and milliners' workshops, a sweet shop and everyday household scenes. A traditional alehouse, De Zwarte Kat (The Black Cat), offers respite for the weary walker.

Cross Rolweg into Carmersstraat and turn right to pass the

Lace is still made the traditional way at the Kantcentrum

Engels Klooster Onze-Lieve-Vrouw van Nazareth (English Convent of Our Lady of Nazareth) at No. 85, founded in 1629 by an order of English Ursuline nuns, with a domed church (1739). The last words of the Flemish poet-priest Guido Gezelle (see page 51), who died here in 1899, are carved on the facade: '…and I was so happy to hear the birds sing'.

Further up Carmersstraat, at 174, is the lodge of the **Schuttersgilde Sint-Sebastiaans** 🟤 (St

Sebastian's Guild; www.sebastiaansgilde.be;). The guild of archers was a powerful, wealthy and influential force in the city, and its sumptuous quarters (16th–17th centuries) reflect this. Inside are a collection of arms and accoutrements, furnishings, gold and silver plate, paintings and other works of art. Among the guild's past members are Belgian royalty, and England's King Charles II – who paid for the banqueting hall – and his brother Henry, both then in exile in Bruges.

Turn right into Kruisvest, where you will see, overlooking the canal, the **Sint-Janshuismolen** (St John's House Windmill; 1770; www.visitbrugge.be). Turn right again into Rolweg, where at No. 64 stands the **Gezellemuseum** ⑰ (www.visitbrugge.be), dedicated to the poet-priest Guido Gezelle (1830–99), in the house where he was born. Surrounded by a large garden, the brick-built, rather gloomy house contains objects related to Gezelle's life and work, including copies of manuscripts and editions of his poetry.

Return to Kruisvest and pass the **Bonne-Chièremolen**, a wooden stilt-windmill, then go right into Stijn Streuvelsstraat. At No. 59 is the lodge of the **Schuttersgilde Sint-Joris** (St George's Guild; www.st-jorisbrugge.be; open by prior arrangement). Unlike the archers of St Sebastian's Guild, St George's members were crossbowmen. Their ornate guild house contains a fine collection of crossbows and the guild's archives. In the garden is a vertical target-mast and walkways protected from descending arrows.

WEST OF JAN VAN EYCKPLEIN

If you return to Jan van Eyckplein you can follow Acadamiestraat from the west side of the square. It joins Vlamingstraat, where at No. 35 you find the elegant **Huis Ter Beurze**. Now serving as a centre for conferences, receptions and exhibitions, the 15th-century house belonged to the Van der Beurze family. They leased rooms to city merchants, who lived and worked in the house; the family's name (rendered as 'bourse' or 'beurs') has come to designate the place for a commercial stock exchange in many languages.

The Genoese merchants in Bruges did their business in the adjacent building. Genuese Loge (Genoese Lodge), dating from 1441, now houses the **Frietmuseum** (Fries Museum; www.frietmuseum. be), dedicated to the humble but tasty – and somewhat misleadingly named – 'French' fries, or chips.

North of the Markt, there are no grand churches to compare with Onze-Lieve-Vrouwekerk or Sint-Salvatorskathedraal, but **Sint-Jakobskerk 18** (St James's Church; summer daily 2–5pm; worshippers only during services) in Sint-Jakobsstraat makes the most determined bid for grandiosity. Thanks to generous gifts from the dukes of Burgundy, the 13th-century Gothic church was improved and enlarged to its present size. It has a pleasing internal harmony lacking in many of the other churches in Bruges, and is illuminated by a pale pink light when the sun is shining. The interior is decorated with an abundance of 16th–18th-century paintings and tombs.

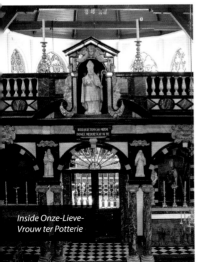

Inside Onze-Lieve-Vrouw ter Potterie

The glorious canopied pulpit is worth a closer inspection for its intricate, skilful carving. Among the most interesting of the tombs is the two-tiered arrangement of Ferry de Gros and his two wives. De Gros, who died in 1544, was a treasurer of the

Order of the Golden Fleece. The tomb is reminiscent of the Italian Renaissance, with ornate floral designs on the ceramic wall-tiles. A walk of less than 1km (0.6 miles) along Ezelstraat leads past the 15th-century **Karmelietenkerk** (Carmelite Church) with its gloomy Baroque interior, to the **Ezelpoort** (Donkey Gate), or **Sint-Jacobspoort** (St James's Gate). One of the four surviving gates of the nine that once allowed passage through the 14th-century city walls, this formidable-looking bastion dates from 1370 and has been rebuilt several times.

NORTH OF JAN VAN EYCKPLEIN

Connected to Woensdagmarkt and Oosterlingenplein is Krom Genthof, a small square on which stands the **Oosterlingenhuis** (Easterners' House; 1481), once the local headquarters of the Hanseatic League, which was trading with Bruges as early as the 13th century. Part of the house survives in what is now the Hotel Bryghia.

For an insight into everyday Bruges, walk across the canal bridge into Potterierei, a different world from the busy city centre. Simply enjoy the peace and quiet, canalside houses, views and bridges. Near the far end of Potterierei a wooden gateway marks the entrance to the **Duinenabdij** (Abbey of the Dunes), a foundation that was based at Koksijde on the North Sea coast until it was forced to retreat from encroaching seas in 1560 and in the 17th century set up here. Since 1833 this has been the Episcopal Seminary.

Continue up Potterierei to No. 79, **Onze-Lieve-Vrouw ter Potterie ⑲** (Our Lady of the Pottery; museum www.museabrugge.be), formerly a hospice, with a recorded history going back to 1276. Most of the complex is now a senior citizens' home, but part of it – including a ward and cloisters dating from the 14th century – has been opened as a museum. The collection includes tapestries,

A paddle boat moored by Damme's windmill

furniture from the 15th–17th centuries, silverware, religious objects and books, and early Flemish paintings. The adjoining 14th-century church, which used to be the Potters' Guild chapel, is a delight, with a Baroque interior containing, among other treasures, a 13th-century statue of Our Lady of the Pottery said to have miraculous powers; and a 16th-century tapestry of the Nativity.

Return along Potterierei to the first bridge, a drawbridge, cross over to Langerei, and keep going south. Turn right into Sint-Gilliskoorstraat, and then left along Lange Raamtstraat to the **Sint-Gilliskerk** (St Giles' Church), built around 1241 in the early Gothic style, but drastically altered in the 15th century, leaving it with three aisles in place of the earlier cruciform shape. Its treasures include a superb organ and a cycle of paintings from 1774 by Bruges artist Jan Garemijn, depicting the history of the Trinitarian Brothers, whose speciality was raising money to ransom Christians captured by Moslem brigands. The artist Hans Memling was buried here in 1494.

EXCURSIONS

After the near perfection of Bruges, any other town in the region can perhaps seem a tad disappointing, but there are several places of interest that you may like to explore on your way to or from the city beginning with Damme. Slightly further afield, but still within easy striking distance of Bruges are Ghent, the World War I battlefields around Ypres (Ieper), and Veurne.

DAMME

The attractive country roads leading to this picturesque village, 7km (4 miles) northeast of Bruges, are lined with pollarded trees, all kinked to the same angle by the prevailing wind that blows across the open countryside. Once the outer port of its larger neighbour, **Damme** ❷⓿ still retains an air of medieval prosperity, with some fine old buildings and excellent restaurants around its marketplace. With a windmill, and skating on the canal in winter (if it ever gets cold enough again), Damme is a picture-postcard Flemish village.

Damme's main street (Kerkstraat) has a delightful **Stadhuis** (Town Hall) built in 1468, with four corner turrets. In front of the building stands a statue of the poet Jacob van Maerlant (1230–96), who wrote his most important works in Damme. The white sandstone facade is adorned with further statues of historic notables including Charles the Bold and

Bruges to Damme

In the summer, you can take a paddleboat canal cruise from the Noorwegse Kaai, on the edge of Bruges, to Damme. Alternatively, a couple of buses a day travel here from the railway station, but be sure to check the timetable before you set out (www.delijn.be). Even better, you can walk or cycle here along the canalside paths.

The eye-catching Stadhuis in Damme

Margaret of York. At one corner, two 'stones of justice' hang from the wall. They used to be tied to the neck or feet of unfortunate women who had given offence in some way, who were then made to parade round the village.

To the right of the building is **De Grote Sterre** (The Great Star), a twin-gabled 15th-century house that was the home of the Spanish governor in the 17th century. Almost destroyed in a storm in 1990, it has undergone extensive restoration. It now houses the tourist information office. Four doors further down is the 15th-century house where the wedding party of Charles the Bold and Margaret of York was held in 1468. Royal weddings were celebrated in lavish style: these festivities lasted for two weeks.

Sint-Janshospitaal (St John's Hospital) is across the road and down from the Stadhuis. Founded in 1249, it includes a Baroque chapel and a museum of paintings, liturgical objects and sacred books. Further up the street and visible from the museum is the

13th-century tower of one of Bruges' prominent beacons, the **Onze-Lieve-Vrouwekerk** (Church of Our Lady). The church has endured many alterations down the centuries, including a fire started in 1578 by soldiers of William of Orange. The tower, gaining its present appearance as a result of partial demolition in 1725, is now the haunt of jackdaws. The separate nave, which has been restored, can be visited in the summer.

DUDZELE

Just north of Bruges, this village beside the Boudewijn Kanaal to Zeebrugge, lies on the route to Lissewege. Pause for a look at the ruined 12th-century Romanesque **tower** at **Sint-Pieters-Bandenkerk** (Church of St Peter in Chains) in the centre. Across the road is a small museum of local history, the **Heemkundigmuseum De Groene Tente** (The Green Tent; www.degroenetente.be).

LISSEWEGE

This pretty village of whitewashed old houses north of Bruges stands along the **Lisseweegs Vaartje**, a narrow canal that in medieval times connected Lissewege and Bruges. In the main square, Onder de Toren, stands the early Gothic **Onze-Lieve-Vrouw-Bezoekingskerk** (Church of Our Lady of the Visitation), dating from 1225–50, with a flat-topped tower 50m (162ft) high, from which a carillon tune occasionally bursts forth. Inside the church are a superb Baroque organ, 17th- and 18th-century paintings, and a replica of a statue of the Madonna and Child destroyed by the Protestants in the 16th century.

ZEEBRUGGE

A visit to the port and coastal resort of **Zeebrugge** ㉑ ('Sea Bruges') should add to your understanding of Bruges. The harbour theme park, **Seafront Zeebrugge** (www.seafront.be), is full

Riding on the sands at De Haan

of interest, especially for children. Among its many maritime attractions are the old West-Hinder lightship; an interactive exhibition on life on, below and beside the sea; and boat tours of the harbour.

DE HAAN

Widely considered the prettiest resort along the Belgian coast, **De Haan** ㉒ (Le Coq in French) is 16km (10 miles) from Bruges. The central area of De Haan, known as De Concessie (The Concession), is filled with Belle Epoque villas, some converted to hotels, others privately owned. De Haan's tourist office is housed in the 1902 **Tramstation** at Koninklijk Plein, which has Art Nouveau lines and later Art Deco features. Close by are two pagoda-like pavilions, now kiosks, built in 1904 for the town's Casino, which was itself built in 1899 and has since been demolished. The **Hotel Des Brasseurs** is another Belle Epoque gem with Art Nouveau elements. Facing it is the domed **Grand Hotel Belle Vue**, opened in the 1920s in what was a private villa. In adjacent Rembrandtlaan a cluster of villas dating from 1925–7 are listed as historic monuments.

From Koninklijk Plein, walk north along Leopoldlaan past the **Hotel Heritage**, the Art Deco **Hotel Astoria** (1930) and the striking **Stadhuis** (Town Hall; 1899), originally the Grand Hôtel du Coq-sur-Mer. After fleeing from Nazi Germany, in 1933 Albert Einstein lived for six months in the **Villa Savoyarde**, in Jean d'Ardennelaan, west of the Town Hall. Parallel to Leopoldlaan is Maria Hendrikalaan; at No. 20 is the Zee-Linde vacation centre (once known as **Hotel Atlanta**), formerly Crown Prince Albert's villa (1901).

With its safe waters and golden sands, De Haan is a popular family resort. Part of the beach, which is lined with open-air café terraces, is designated for windsurfing. Just west of the resort, golfers play the 18-hole links course of the **Koninklijke Golf Club Oostende** (Royal Ostend Golf Club; www.rogc.eu), bordered by the **Natuurreservaat De Kijkuit** (De Kijkuit Nature Reserve; www.natuurpunt.be) and its protected sand dunes.

OOSTENDE (OSTEND)

Oostende ㉓, the 'Queen of the Coast' and Belgium's liveliest North Sea resort, is quickly reached by train from Bruges. Outside its

THE COAST TRAM

Belgium's North Sea coastline stretches 64km (40 miles) from the Dutch to the French border. Access to the entire coast is made easy by the *Kusttram* (Coast Tram), which in two hours runs almost the full length of the shore, between Knokke-Heist and De Panne. It is one of the world's longest tramlines, with 67km (42 miles) of tracks. These pass through chic Knokke-Heist, the busy port of Zeebrugge, the yacht harbour at Blankenberge, Belle Epoque De Haan, bustling Ostend, the fishing harbour of Nieuwpoort and the long beaches of Oostduinkerke and De Panne. For a considerable part of the way the tram runs along just behind the sand dunes; on other stretches it plunges into busy towns like Ostend and Zeebrugge. You can use it either as a touring option or as a straightforward, fast way to get from one place to another. The *Kusttram* is operated by the public transport company of Flanders, De Lijn (www.delijn.be/dekusttram).

splendid railway station stands a reminder of the town's maritime heritage. The green-hulled **Amandine** (www.amandineoostende. be), built in 1961, ended her Arctic voyaging in 1995. This last of Ostend's Iceland-bound trawlers is now permanently 'moored' at the edge of the harbour, in a dry basin. Adjacent **Visserskaai** (Fishermen's Wharf) is lined with seafood restaurants and seafood stalls. Here also is the **Vistrap** (Fish Market), where the day's trawler catch is sold.

Post-war apartment blocks line Albert I Promenade, replacing demolished 19th-century mansions on the once-fashionable seafront esplanade. Turn left into Vlaanderenstraat, to the 19th-century **Ensorhuis** (www.ensorhuis.be), at No. 27, where the Anglo-Belgian painter James Ensor lived from 1916 until his death in 1949. In Ensor's time, this attractive town house had a souvenir shop on the ground floor and his studio on the first. Continuing beside the beach brings you to the **Casino-Kursaal** (www.kursaal-oostende.be), a 1950s replacement for an 1887 original blown up by the Germans in World War II. In addition to gaming tables, there are restaurants and cafés.

You now reach the 19th-century **Venetiaanse Gaanderijen** (Venetian Galleries). At the entrance to this former royal pavilion is a bronze sculpture of King Baudouin (1951–93), on foot and wearing a raincoat, on a visit to Ostend. Albert I Promenade joins the Zeedijk (Sea Dike) as you come face to face with an equestrian statue (dating from 1931) of that brutal colonialist King Leopold II (1865–1909). Adjacent to this begins the long **Koninklijke Gaanderijen** (Royal Galleries), built in 1906 by French architect Charles Girault so that Leopold II and his court could shelter from the wind as they passed along the seafront. The plush Art Deco Thermae Palace hotel in the middle dates from 1933.

Head east on Koningin Astridlaan and Warschauwstraat to Leopold I Plein, with its **equestrian statue** of King Leopold I

(1831–65). If you are interested in modern art, you could make a long trek south on Rogierlaan, then into Romestraat to the **Kunst Museum aan Zee** (Art Museum by the Sea; www.muzee.be) at No. 11. In this converted Modernist department store you can see mostly Belgian works by the likes of Panamarenko and Jan Fabre. Take Witte Nonnenstraat to Wapenplein, a square with a wrought-iron bandstand in the middle.

At the end of Kerkstraat is the colossal neo-Gothic edifice **of Sint-Petrus-en-Pauluskerk** (Church of Sts Peter and Paul). Inside is the tomb of Belgium's first queen, Marie-Louise of Orléans, who died in Ostend in 1850. Back at the harbour, on Jan Piersplein, the yacht harbour hosts the elegant, three-masted schooner **Mercator** (www.zeilschipmercator.be), a merchant marine training ship that spends most of its time here as a floating museum.

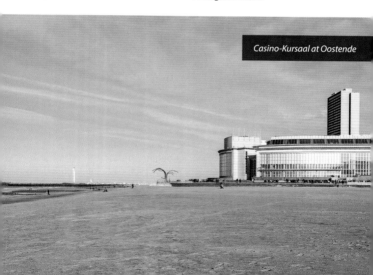

Casino-Kursaal at Oostende

VEURNE

Just 6km (4 miles) from the border with France is the small town of **Veurne ㉔**, with a population not much greater than that of Damme. Veurne grew from a 9th-century fortress and now has an attractive central marketplace, among the prettiest in Belgium. The town's *Boetprocessie* (Procession of the Penitents) takes place on the last Sunday in July, presenting scenes from Christ's Passion. Owing much to Spanish influence (the town once served as a Spanish garrison), the procession is similar to the Spanish celebration of *Semana Santa* (Holy Week). Other processions are staged during Easter and Lent.

Most of Veurne's places of interest are in or alongside the central **Grote Markt**, where you will also find plenty of cafés and restaurants. In the summer months, tickets for guided tours through the town are available from the tourist office in the square.

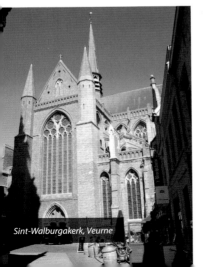

Sint-Walburgakerk, Veurne

The typical yellow Flemish brick is much in evidence, together with an architectural style that shows a restrained Spanish influence. The gabled **Stadhuis** (Town Hall) in the Grote Markt, built in 1612, has an attractive loggia of bluestone contrasting with the yellow brick of the rest of the structure. Visitors can join guided tours of the interior, which features some unusual and impressive leather wall hangings originating from Córdoba in southern Spain.

The **Landhuis**, adjoining the Stadhuis, was built in 1616, its Gothic bell-tower topped with a Baroque spire. It houses the tourist information office. Next door is a delightful parade of five houses with step gables, each with a different design of columns around the windows. The cafés on the ground floors spill out into the square on warm days. On the northeast side of the square is the **Spaans Paviljoen** (Spanish Pavilion), which as the name suggests, was the headquarters for Spanish officers during the 17th century. Across the road, the building with all the window shutters is the Renaissance **Vleeshuis** (Meat Market), built in 1615, and now a library.

The imposing tower of **Sint-Niklaaskerk** (Church of St Nicholas), rising from nearby Appelmarkt, can be climbed to get a good view; the 13th-century structure has a carillon. The other church in the town is **Sint-Walburgakerk** (Church of St Walpurga), construction of which began in 1250 with ambitious plans that eventually proved too much for the little town. It has a splendid 27m (90ft) nave. The interior of the church is worth a visit, more for its overall effect than for any specific item, though there is a fine Baroque pulpit.

YPRES AND FLANDERS FIELDS

Southwest of Bruges towards the border with France lies **Flanders Fields**, a pocket-sized agricultural area that witnessed military carnage on what was then an unprecedented scale. Although the senseless waste of millions of lives in World War I has gone down in history, the staggering numbers killed nevertheless still have the power to shock. Row upon row of gravestones in the many cemeteries of the area testify to the butchery of war. Whether or not you have relatives buried here, the peacefulness of the place and the solidarity in death of troops from all sides make for a moving and strangely comforting experience – the soldiers' ordeal is at an end.

Ypres 25 (Ieper) is a name that still resonates in collective memory. The focus of repeated attacks and counter-attacks, it was shelled to destruction during World War I, then carefully reconstructed over the next 40 years. Nothing old remains in the bustling town, but it has an open, relaxed central Grote Markt and an imposing Stadhuis. The **In Flanders Fields Museum** (www. inflandersfields.be) is a striking interactive museum located in the reconstructed **Lakenhalle** (Cloth Hall). It uses historical documents, film footage, poetry, song and sound effects to evoke the brutal experience of trench warfare in the **Ypres Salient**.

The **Menin Gate** memorial, located just off the Grote Markt, is built on a gateway through which thousands of men made their way towards the Ypres Salient. Designed by Reginald Blomfield, it comprises a classical facade fronting a vast arch with three open ceiling oculi. It is inscribed with the names of nearly 55,000 British soldiers who died in battle but have no known graves.

Every evening at 8pm, the Last Post is played here by local volunteer buglers to commemorate those who died. This ceremony has taken place every evening since July 1928, except for the

TOURS OF REMEMBRANCE

There are coach tours available from Bruges that visit selected towns, war cemeteries and memorials. Alternatively, if you wish to take more time and follow your own inclinations, it is worth taking a car (or even a bicycle) and making use of 'Route 14–18', a sign-posted route through the battlefield area of the Ypres Salient. It should be stressed, however, that nothing much remains of the battlefields. Where you wish to go will depend on any family connections you may have with the war, and our survey of sites is necessarily selective.

period when the city was occupied by the German army during World War II.

THE WAR CEMETERIES

On Hill 62, just southeast of Ypres near Zillebeke, stands a memorial to the Canadian troops who lost their lives. Near the hill, **Sanctuary Wood Cemetery** preserves a few remaining sections of trench. At Hill 60, a little further beyond Zillebeke, a roadside memorial commemorates the fallen of Australia, behind which lies a field of mounds and hollows, created by intensive bombardment, where you can still make out the ruins of bunkers. This 'strategically important' hill was constantly taken and retaken throughout World War I. Today, sheep graze here and birds sing in the trees.

A little over 10km (6 miles) northeast of Ypres, situated off the N332 before Passendale (Passchendaele), is **Tyne Cot**

Tyne Cot is the largest military cemetery in Flanders

Commonwealth War Graves Cemetery ㉖. Designed by the architect Sir Herbert Baker, the cemetery was intended to evoke the appearance of a traditional English graveyard, with white gravestones standing honourably in regular formation on a neat green lawn. Its large Cross of Sacrifice in Portland stone is built on the site of the Tyne Cot dressing station that was finally captured by Australian troops in 1917. The slight rise on which the cemetery is located affords a view over the now peaceful countryside.

The German cemetery located at **Langemark**, approximately 16km (10 miles) north of Ypres, contains the remains of more than 44,000 German soldiers – over half of them in a mass grave. It is referred to as the Students' Cemetery because so many young soldiers perished in the Ypres Salient in 1914 and 1915. The gravestones are simple tablets that lie flush with the lawn, on ground sheltered by mature trees. The cemetery contains the remnants of three bunkers.

Further northwest, 4km (2.5 miles) outside the town of Diksmuide, **Vladslo** German cemetery is the site of more than 25,000 German graves and an extremely moving memorial sculpture by Käthe Kollwitz (1867–1945) entitled *Grieving Parents*. The German sculptor's younger son, Peter, killed in October 1914, lies buried there.

In fact, there are more than 150 war cemeteries in this area.

SINT-ANDRIES

Two large country estates are embedded in the forests a short distance southwest of Bruges, in the city's **Sint-Andries** ➋ suburb. **Domein Beisbroek** has a **Natuurcentrum** (Nature Centre; free), a **Volkssterrenwacht** (Observatory; www.cozmix.be; open for pre-arranged groups) and the **Zeiss Planetarium,** which explains the mysteries of the night sky.

At nearby **Domein Tudor** the splendid neo-Gothic **Kasteel Tudor** (Tudor Castle; www.kasteeltudor.be), built in 1904, is run as a celebrations room and seminar centre.

TILLEGEMBOS

Take bus No. 25, alight at 'Vozelzang' stop, and walk 900m along Kervyndreef to the woods of **Tillegembos** ➋ in Bruges' southwestern suburb, Sint-Michiels. The woods cover an area of 80 hectares (200 acres), providing a rural retreat from the city. Lots of well-marked footpaths lead you around this former estate, and there is also a lakeside inn, a picturesque mill and play areas for children. The on-site moated **Kasteel Tillegem**, a fortress dating from the 14th century, is the headquarters of the West Flanders Province and only open during heritage days (ask tourist board).

KASTEEL LOPPEM

Situated just 3km (2 miles) south of Bruges is the neo-Gothic **Kasteel Loppem** ➋ (www.kasteelvanloppem.be). It was conceived by Augustus Pugin, architect of the British Houses of Parliament, and later completed by Jean Béthune. Built between 1858 and 1863, the house is sumptuously decorated; the tone dominated by the wood of the ceilings and furniture, as well as numerous artworks. It has a private chapel and a wonderful, soaring hall, and the extensive gardens feature a 19th-century hedge labyrinth for children to explore.

GHENT

Ghent ❸ (Gent in Dutch), lies at the confluence of the rivers Scheldt and Leie. The city is a little larger than Bruges, but most of its historic attractions are clustered together within walking distance of one another. It is a city built on diverse economic interests, with the sense to preserve its historical heart. That past is shown in some magnificent buildings spread along canals, second only to those of Bruges in splendour. Quaint trams trundle

WHO PAINTED THE ALTERPIECE?

Whether or not van Eyck really was responsible for *The Adoration of the Mystic Lamb* has been a matter of some dispute. An inscription on the frame of the altarpiece declares that it was started by his brother Hubert van Eyck and completed by Jan. However, since no-one has any other evidence for the existence of Hubert, it is thought by many that he was the mythical creation of Ghent citizens jealous of Bruges' monopolising of Jan. Certainly, it is difficult to believe that an artist of van Eyck's genius could be surpassed by someone who has otherwise left nothing to posterity. Most art historians today unhesitatingly attribute the work of this painting solely to the master artist Jan van Eyck.

through the cobbled centre of this inland port city, which has a lively, jaunty air about it thanks to the tables of cafés and bars spilling out onto the pavements.

Our tour starts from Sint-Baafsplein. Most of Ghent's historic centre lies northwest of this square, straddling the Y-shaped meeting of the two rivers. This area is one of winding streets and alleyways, while the south is lined with elegant boulevards and imposing mansions.

Houses along Ghent's Korenlei

SINT-BAAFSKATHEDRAAL

The largely Gothic **Sint-Baafskathedraal** Ⓐ (St Bavo's Cathedral; www.sintbaafskathedraal.be) was constructed over the course of several centuries. The chancel dates from the turn of the 14th century, both the tower and the nave from the 15th century, and the transept from the mid-16th century. In the nave, a forest of stone leads the eye upwards to a glorious late-Gothic display of rib vaulting in the roof. The tower contains a carillon, and the crypt retains some of the structure of an earlier Romanesque church.

Accessed via a separate entrance in the north transept, the cathedral's greatest treasure dominates a side chapel at the back of the ambulatory. This marvellous panel painting, variously known as the *Ghent Altarpiece* or *The Adoration of the Mystic Lamb*, is regarded as the crowning achievement of Jan van Eyck's Gothic style, which instituted a new kind of realism.

The altarpiece seems to become increasingly detailed the closer you look at it, and the painting is invested with humanity and optimism, with God the Father looking kindly upon it all. If you look carefully, you will see Bruges Cathedral in the background of the central panel.

There are many other important works of art in the cathedral. Rubens' painting of 1624, *The Conversion of St Bavo*, is full of the unique drama with which the artist infused all his work. Also of interest is Frans Pourbus the Elder's *Christ Among the Doctors*, painted in 1571. A youthful Jesus is shown amazing the elders of the temple with his knowledge and wisdom, but it is his audience that claims our attention: Pourbus portrayed contemporary luminaries such as Philip II and Charles V, Thomas Calvin, and even his rival, painter Pieter Brueghel the Elder in the crowd. Down in the crypt is the striking *Calvary Triptych* of Justus van Gent, painted in 1466.

You will also find splendid examples of sculpture, the best of which is the Baroque oak and marble pulpit, one of Laurent Delvaux's masterpieces, completed in 1741. The dynamic, intricate carving of the design sweeps the eye up to where the preacher would stand, above which an ornate marble tree of knowledge grows complete with exquisitely gilded serpent and fruit. St Bavo himself is commemorated in the Baroque high altar of sculptor Hendrik Frans Verbruggen.

Tourist office

Ghent's tourist office (www.visitgent.be) is based inside the renovated Oude Vismijn (Old Fish Market) on Sint-Veerleplein. It is open daily Apr–Sept 9.30am–6.30pm, Oct–Mar 9.30am–4.30pm.

THE BELFORT AND LAKENHALLE

Opposite the cathedral, the **Belfort**  (Belfry; www.visitgent.be), completed in 1380, has since become the pre-eminent symbol of the city's independence and houses one of the best carillons in Belgium. You can view the 53 bells on the fifth floor using the glass lift and ascend to the top of the 91m (298ft) tower for spectacular views across the city.

The towering Belfry

The gilded copper dragon at the top of the spire was first installed upon completion of the tower, but the creature and the four figures now poised at the corners of the viewing platform are modern replicas. The spire itself was restored at the beginning of the 20th century according to the original 14th-century design.

In front, stands the ultra-modern steel-and-wood Stadshal – a popular meeting place and rallying point. see page 105).

The neighbouring **Lakenhalle** (Cloth Hall) is another display of Ghent's civic pride and bygone wealth. The building, much restored, dates from 1441, once serving as the headquarters of the city's wool and cloth traders.

BOTERMARKT AND HOOGPOORT

Across the road from the Lakenhalle in Botermarkt stands the **Stadhuis** ⊙ (Town Hall; guided visits only). All pilasters and windows, the Stadhuis is like a catalogue of architecture: the oldest part of the building (on the Hoogpoort side) dates from the early 16th century and, with its florid design and ornate statues, follows the style of Bruges' Stadhuis. Religious disputes in 1539 and the economic decline of Ghent halted the work for some 60 years. Work began again with the Renaissance-style facade of the Botermarkt side of the hall; it was continued in the 18th century with the Baroque facade facing the corner of Hoogpoort and Stadhuissteeg and the rococo Poeljemarkt side. The throne room and an impressive city council room are accessible to visitors on guided tours. Don't miss the Stadshal on Poeljemarkt, a modern counterpoint to the nearby historical buildings. This multifunctional architectural gem is made of glass, wood and concrete and hosts concerts, dance performances and markets. It makes for an excellent meeting point or refreshment stop.

North from St Baafsplein, Hoogpoort runs northwest past some beautiful Ghent houses. On the corner with the square stands **Sint-Jorishof**, the former house of the Guild of Crossbowmen, built in 1477. It was here that Mary of Burgundy granted a charter of freedoms to the Flemish cloth towns. Hoogpoort leads to Groentenmarkt, site of the medieval pillory and former vegetable market. The **Groot Vleeshuis**, on the west side of the square, comprises a complex of gabled buildings restored in 1912 but dating from 1406. The buildings is currently closed for a major refurbishment.

The Korenmarkt (Corn Market) connects via Kortemunt with Groentenmarkt; at its southern end stands the landmark **Sint-Niklaaskerk** ⑩ (St Nicholas' Church), from where Sint-Michielsbrug (St Michael's

Canal Cruises

Like Bruges, Ghent offers canal boat cruises in summer. It is also fun to tour the city by tram: the main tram terminus is outside Sint-Pieters train station.

Cruising along Korenlei

Bridge) spans the Leie River. The oldest parts of the Gothic Sint-Niklaaskerk date back to the 13th century, but the building was not completed until five centuries later. Inside, the Baroque high altar is a typically energetic design of the period. The whole church is flooded with a beautiful light on sunny days.

This area offers some of the most characteristic views of Ghent from Sint-Michielsbrug; you can make out the towers of the Belfry and Sint-Baaf's Cathedral, the picturesque Korenlei and Graslei quaysides, and the ominous mass of Gravensteen, the Castle of the Counts. Across from the bridge you will see **Sint-Michielskerk** (St Michael's Church), which acts as a kind of visual counterbalance to Sint-Niklaaskerk.

KORENLEI AND GRASLEI

North from Sint-Michielsbrug, you can stroll on both banks of the river, past a splendid array of medieval guild houses on the

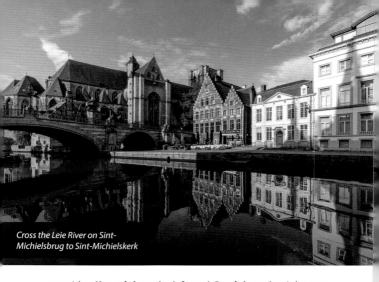

Cross the Leie River on Sint-Michielsbrug to Sint-Michielskerk

quaysides. **Korenlei**, on the left, and **Graslei**, on the right, comprise Ghent's oldest harbour, the **Tussen Bruggen** (Between the Bridges). This area was the commercial heart of the medieval city and the place where Ghent's wealthy guilds eventually chose to build.

Along Korenlei, a building to watch out for is the **Gildehuis van de Onvrije Schippers** (House of the Tied Boatmen), at No. 7, built in 1739, an excellent example of Flemish Baroque, with spectacular dolphins and lions adorning the gables and a gilded ship crowning the roof. Another is the 16th-century **De Zwane** (The Swan) at No. 9, a former brewery that has a graceful swan depicted in two carvings on the gables.

Look over the water to Graslei for a view of the even finer houses on that quay before crossing for a closer inspection. The **Gildehuis van de Vrije Schippers** (House of the Free Boatmen) was built in 1531, in Brabant Gothic style, while next door, the second Baroque

Gildehuis van de Graanmeters (House of the Grain Weighers) dates back to 1698.

The little **Tolhuisje** (Customs House), built in 1682, looks like an attractive Renaissance afterthought. Next door is the Romanesque-style **Het Spijker**, also known as Koornstapelhuis (a former grain warehouse), dating from about 1200, and the adjacent **Korenmetershuis** (Corn Measurer's house), followed by the Gothic **Gildehuis van de Metselaars** (House of the Masons), dating from 1527 and also built in Brabant Gothic style.

NORTH OF KORENLEI

Jan Breydelstraat branches off from the north end of Korenlei. At No. 5, occupying a house built in 1755 by the De Coninck family, is the **Design Museum Gent** E (www.designmuseumgent.be). This is devoted to interior design and furnishings including a number of period rooms decorated in 18th-century style. There is also a wonderful Art Nouveau collection, the best in the country, and some fine examples of Art Deco, as well as more modern pieces.

Further along, in neighbouring Burgstraat, the Renaissance-gabled house decorated with portraits of the Counts of Flanders is the **Huis der Gekroonde Hoofden** (House of the Crowned Heads), now housing a restaurant of the same name.

GRAVENSTEEN

Proceeding along Rekelingestraat, you soon reach the heavily renovated fortress called **Het Gravensteen** F (Castle of the Counts; https://gravensteen.stad.gent/en). The

CityCard Ghent

Valid for 48 or 72 hours, the CityCard Ghent grants free entry to all Ghent's historic sites and museums. It costs €38/44 and can be bought online or at the tourist information office (www.visitgent.be).

castle is still a powerful and ominous presence here, with massive fortifications comprising crenellated cylindrical towers and a vast brooding keep.

Work began on the structure in 1180 on the site of a 9th-century castle, on the orders of Philip of Alsace. The building was closely modelled on the Crusader castles of the Holy Land; a climb along the battlements provides excellent views and a welcome blast of fresh air. A large and dark gateway leads to the central courtyard, which is surrounded by turreted walls, and the central keep may be explored via a spiral staircase. Inside, the keep contains the living quarters of a succession of Counts of Flanders, including the impressive Great Hall where Philip the Good fêted the Knights of the Golden Fleece in 1445.

FROM KRAANLEI TO VRIJDAGMARKT

Kraanlei is lined with fine houses; at No. 65 the almshouses are now home to **Huis van Alijn** (Alijn House; www.huisvanalijn.be), the city's folklore museum. Built in 1363, this beautifully restored complex is comprised of 18 interconnected cottages arranged around a courtyard. Each room is decorated in typical 1900 style. The everyday life of working people is evoked through the items and tools they would have known and used and the few luxuries they could afford.

Crossing the Leie via the Zuivelbrug leads to Grootkannonplein, where you will meet **Dulle Griet** (Mad Meg); a 16-tonne cannon made in the 15th century, standing on the quayside, supported by three stone plinths.

Just a few steps away, **Vrijdagmarkt** (Friday Market) has some excellent examples of guild houses, with a 19th-century statue of Ghent hero Jacob van Artevelde at the centre of the square. The stylish Art Nouveau building named **Ons Huis**, which was built in 1900, used to belong to the Socialist Workers' Association; it is attractive in itself, though it appears too tall for the square. Older houses include Nos 22 and 43–7, built in the 17th and 18th centuries respectively.

In this square the Flemish Counts were sworn in by the citizens of the city. Visible from the square at Koningstraat 18, the **Koninklijke Vlaamse Academie voor Taal** (Royal Flemish Academy for Languages) is an imposing Baroque mansion that looms

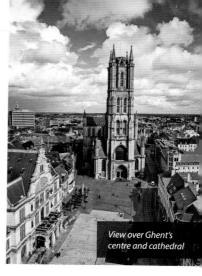

View over Ghent's centre and cathedral

over the entire length of the street. A short walk north-east from here, on Minnemeers 10, is the excellent interactive Museum of Industry, Work and Textile (MIAT; www.industriemuseum.be). Housed in an old cotton mill by the River Leie, the museum is spread over five floors, and documents technological manufacturing changes of the last 250 years. Exhibitions include old textile machinery as well as an interesting, if slightly sobering, section on child labour. The museum also boasts wide views across the city from upper floors.

AROUND VELDSTRAAT

Veldstraat, running south from Sint-Niklaaskerk, is the city's main shopping street, as you will soon realise from the crowds (the street is pedestrianised). Many of the original building exteriors remain. The most flamboyant of these, at no.55, is the **Hotel d'Hane-Steenhuyse** (www.visitgent.be). The eye-catching rococo facade of this 18th-century mansion is matched by the interior, an immaculately preserved affair complete wih frescoes and a galleried ball room. An obese King Louis XVIII of France lived here briefly when he fled from Napoleon; other inhabitants have included the French writer and statesman Talleyrand and members of the Russian royal family.

Across the street, at No. 82, the **Museum Arnold Vander Haeghen** (www.visitgent.be) is devoted to the library of Nobel Prize-winning writer Maurice Maeterlinck (1862–1949) and Ghent graphic artist Victor Stuyvaert. The house was built in 1741; in 1815 it was home to the Duke of Wellington. It has a charming Chinese salon with silk wallpaper and some 18th- and 19th-century interior designs; it also hosts a variety of temporary exhibitions.

Turn left at Zonnestraat to **Kouter** and you will find yourself in a large square that has fair claim to being the most historically significant one in the city. A variety of festivals, military parades, political demonstrations, meetings, archery contests and tournaments have taken place here through the centuries, and a flower market has been held in the square on Sunday since the 18th century. It may be difficult to envisage all the pomp of the past, as very few buildings of any antiquity have survived; exceptions to this are the house at No. 29 and the Opera House, situated off the square in Schouwburgstraat, and completed in 1840.

FINE ARTS MUSEUMS

A 10-minute walk along Charles de Kerchovelaan leads to **Citadelpark**, a large chunk of greenery, which takes its name from the fortress that stood here until the 1870s, when the land was cleared and prettified with the addition of grottoes and ponds, statues and fountains, a waterfall and a bandstand. These nineteenth-century niceties survive today and, as an added bonus, a network of footpaths crisscross the park. Even better, if you have spent much time in Ghent, which is almost universally flat,

Citadelpark seems refreshingly hilly. In the eastern corner of the park is the **Museum voor Schone Kunsten**  (Museum of Fine Arts; www.mskgent.be). The strange art of Hieronymus Bosch is represented by *Christ Carrying the Cross*, an unforgettable painting showing Christ on the way to Calvary.

Among other Flemish and Dutch exhibits are works by Jacob Jordaens, Frans Hals' bravura *Old Lady* – full of exuberant brushwork – Pieter Brueghel the Younger's *Peasant Wedding* and a rather harassed *Village Advocate*. Rubens is represented by a *Scourging of Christ* and *St Francis Receiving the Stigmata*. Later paintings include works by Géricault, Corot, Courbet, Daumier, Ensor and Rouault. The former casino opposite the Museum of Fine Arts is now occupied by **SMAK** (Museum of Contemporary Art; www.smak.be). The permanent collection is mainly devoted to Belgian and international artists since 1945, with works by Bacon, Panamarenko, Broodthaers, Long and Nauman. The museum also has a reputation for outstanding temporary exhibitions.

Just north of the Leie canal, at Godshuizenlaan 2, is **STAM** (Stadmuseum Gent; www.stamgent.be), a dynamic museum outlining the city's history. It occupies part of the site where the former Cistercian **Bijlokeabdij** (Bijloke Abbey) has stood from the thirteenth century. Much of

STAM, Ghent City Museum

HOW FLANDERS INFLUENCED ART

Medieval Flanders bequeathed some of the most profound and best-loved paintings to the world, the greatest of which can be seen in Bruges and Ghent. The brilliance of painters such as Bosch, Memling and van Eyck sprang from the Gothic tradition that nurtured them. Gothic art was essentially a religious art form, with devotional paintings depicting the life of Christ, the Virgin Mary and the saints, but in Flanders it also came to place great emphasis on the accurate representation of the world, which was seen as God's creation and a vehicle for the sacred.

Van Eyck retained the religious subject matter of the Gothic tradition, but used the revolutionary medium of oil, enabling him to paint with greater control. No artist before him had observed nature so minutely, or was capable of rendering observations so precisely. His paintings (including his *Madonna and Child with Canon Joris van der Paele*, in Bruges, and the famous *Ghent Altarpiece*, in Sint-Baafskathedraal), along with those of Memling and artists such as Hugo van der Goes and Pieter Pourbus, reinforce this truthfulness to appearance.

The combination of sacred theme and faithful depiction of the world was taken a stage further a hundred years after van Eyck in the work of Brueghel the Elder, whose paintings of biblical events are set in the recognisable peasant world of his time.

Nevertheless, the genius of an artist usually needs fertile soil in which to grow. For a long time the wealth of the Burgundian court and the merchant class of Bruges and Ghent was enough to pay for the commissioning of new works.

Eventually, however, the economic centre of gravity moved northward to Antwerp (home to Rubens and his pupil Van Dyck) and the Netherlands, where the first sophisticated market for genre paintings developed.

the medieval complex has survived and, with subsequent additions, now occupies a sprawling multi-use site. A visit to STAM begins in a bright, modern cube-like structure and continue in the former abbey church and cloisters, with one of the early highlights being the two delightful medieval wall paintings in the old refectory. Look out also for the room full of medieval illuminated books, incidental sculpture and a selection of vintage military hardware.

Sint-Pieterskerk

SINT-PIETERSPLEIN

North of the museum, Overpoortstraat leads to Sint-Pietersplein, where there are regular exhibitions of art and other cultural events at the **Kunsthal Sint-Pietersabdij** (St Peter's Abbey Arts Centre; www.visitgent.be).

The splendid 57m (188ft) cupola of **Onze-Lieve-Vrouw Sint-Pieterskerk** ⓗ (Church of Our Lady of St Peter) can be seen for many streets around. The Baroque church was designed by the Huyssens brothers and built in 1719. Clearly, the architects were not lacking in ambition: the design is based on St Peter's Basilica in Rome. The impressive facade dominates attractive Sint-Pietersplein; the church has an exuberant Baroque-style interior and artworks by Van Dyck. From Sint-Pietersplein, Sint-Kwintensberg leads to Nederkouter, and then Veldstraat.

Take a ride around Bruges in a horse-drawn carriage

THINGS TO DO

SHOPPING

The thought of shopping in Bruges may not immediately leap to mind, but the city has a large range of stores of all descriptions. Bruges is adapted to the lucrative tourist trade so you will find plenty of specialised stores and souvenirs. Except for certain items, such as chocolates or lace, prices are probably what you would expect to pay at home.

WHERE TO SHOP

The main shopping street is Steenstraat, off the Markt, which has everything you would expect in the way of shops catering to everyday local needs, including clothes, shoes, food, home furnishings and electrical goods. There are also a few shops that sell Belgian chocolates and souvenirs. The street and its associated malls become very crowded on Saturday, when the best time to go is first thing in the morning.

Bruges' network of small city-centre streets and alleys conceals a surprising number of shops, most of them specialising in items such as lace, chocolate or clothes. Particular streets to look around are those surrounding the Burg and the Markt. Most of the city's squares have few shops: the Markt and the Burg are bounded

> **Shopping hours**
>
> Shopping hours are 9/10am–5.30/6pm; some smaller shops close for an hour at lunch time. Late-night shopping tends to be on Friday, with many stores open until 7–7.30pm. Shops that cater mainly to tourists, which in Bruges is just about all of them, usually open on Sunday.

by historical buildings with some cafés and restaurants; Jan van Eyckplein has none; and 't Zand is all bistros and hotels.

Bruges has a number of markets. The main one is on Wednesday on the Markt, and there is a bric-a-brac and craft market on 't Zand and Beursplein on Saturday (both open 8am–1pm). Don't miss the excellent antiques and flea market that takes place along the Dijver canal from 15 March to 15 November on Saturday and Sunday from 10am–6pm. A huge flea market is held three times a year (in August and September) in Koning Albertpark and 't Zand Square.

GOOD BUYS

Antiques. These are plentiful and are sold mostly in small, expensive-looking stores in the narrow side streets off the main shopping areas. An excellent example is Antiek Theatergalerij (Atelier Papageno, Vlamingstraat 52; tel: www.antiek-vanmullem.be), which deals in restored old furniture, chandeliers and paintings.

Beer. This is an essential purchase for connoisseurs, with many brands on sale that are simply not available abroad. You will need a car to carry significant quantities. The range of Belgian beers is vast, so it is safest to stick to those you have tried and liked rather than risk being disappointed by an unknown. Note that it is much cheaper to buy beer at conventional supermarkets, but they may not stock your favourites. A good place to try in Bruges is the Bottle Shop at Wollestraat 13 (www.thebottleshop.be), which stocks local beers and dozens of others.

Tax-free?

Tax-free shopping is available in stores that display the appropriate notice – usually the larger or more expensive specialised stores. If you're not sure, ask for details in the shop itself (see also page 121).

Exquisite handmade chocolates are everywhere

Chocolate. 'Made in Belgium', probably the best in the world and available everywhere. It is best to avoid the tourist-oriented products, such as the chocolate rabbits, and concentrate on the incomparable delights of the classic, exquisite, handmade Belgian praline and truffle. Selection boxes (either pre-packed, or filled with your own choices) can be bought in a range of weights and are always attractively gift-wrapped.

A good shop in Bruges is Chocolatier Van Oost at Wollestraat 11 (www.chocolatiervanoost.com), a small store with a select range. Other fine outlets worth visiting are Pralinette, at Wollestraat 31B (www.pralinette.be), and The Chocolate Line, at Simon Stevinplein 19 (www.thechocolateline.be).

Food and wine. Purchases may be limited by your tastes and appetites, the time of year, the freshness of the produce, or even the size of your car. But it would be a shame not to come away with something, even if it is just for your return journey. Belgium is justly

Jenever gin, known as Dutch gin by the English, is Belgium's national spirit

€ 17,36   € 17,36

celebrated for its pâtisseries and cakes, and there are some superb specialist food shops and delicatessens in Bruges.

Vintage clothes Bruges boasts a scattering of second-hand clothes shops, but easily the pick is Think Twice (T2), whose adventurous, well-chosen items – for both men and women – are on display at their city centre premises at Vlamingstraat 25 (www.thinktwice-secondhand.be).

Lace. Lace was once Bruges' principal product and is certainly the premier souvenir today. In the course of your strolls through the city you are likely to see enough lace shops to satisfy even the most ardent admirer of this delicate fabric. Although most lace on sale today is machine-made, usually in the Far East, handmade lace in the distinctive *duchesse* (duchess), *bloemenwerk* (flower lace), *rozenkant* (pearled rosary), and *toveressesteek* (fairy stitch) styles can still be found. Some shops deal exclusively in the handmade product, which has a Quality Control label and is, of course, more expensive, but most shops sell a mix of the two. Breidelstraat (connecting the Markt with the Burg) is the city's lace alley and a tourist favourite, but it is sold throughout the city, so you will have plenty of choice. Reliable sources of guaranteed, authentic Belgian handmade lace are the family-run Lace Jewel, at Philipstockstraat 11 (www.bruges-shop.com), and, the pick of the lot, 't Apostelientje, at Balstraat 11 (www.apostelientje.be).

ENTERTAINMENT

Walking, watching, eating and drinking are the chief pleasures of Bruges, but you can tour the city by boat and by horse-drawn carriage – peaceful and relaxing ways to see the sights (see page 117).

Bookmark 4,50

Handmade Belgian lace

Bruges' café scene mainly takes place indoors, since space and city preservation rules allow little else (although tables do appear outside in the summer, and some pedestrianised squares, like little Huidenvettersplein, provide exceptions to this rule).

Bicycles are easy to rent (see page 110) and the city is flat, though you will have to cope with the cobblestones. From Bruges, you can easily cycle to Damme along the canal.

NIGHTLIFE

Music, opera, theatre. There are regular music festivals and concerts throughout the year; the city tourist office will have the latest information. Bruges has performances of classical music, opera and dance at the Concertgebouw, in 't Zand, and at the Stadsschouwburg, Vlamingstraat 29 (www.ccbrugge.be). Churches

Bars and restaurants in the Markt

frequently host a variety of concerts and recitals too.

Cinemas. International films are shown in their original language, with subtitles. The tourist office in Bruges can tell you what's on; the main cinema is Lumière at Sint-Jacobsstraat 36 (www.

lumiere-brugge.be), while Liberty in Kuipersstraat 23 (www.cine news.be) has the occasional off-beat film.

Nightclubs. In Ghent, most clubs are to be found in the Zuid Quarter, but Bruges has little to offer those who want to dance the night away; it tends to be quiet at night. The Cactus Club, Werfstraat 108 (www. cactusmusic.be), on the north side of the city centre, is one of Bruges' most adventurous venues, with its electro-industrial and frontline-assembly bands, as well as nostalgia events like rock-and-roll dances.

The lounge-bar Lio's, in the Oud Sint-Jan complex between Mariastraat and Zonnekemeers (www.liosbrugge.be), has regular DJ evenings. In equally hip Lokkedize, Korte Vulderstraat 33 (http://bistrolokkedize.be), one can hear jazz, blues and rock'n'roll.

Bars. 't Brugs Beertje, a popular and traditional bar-café at Kemelstraat 5 (www.brugsbeertje.be), has more than 300 ales on its menu. Old World atmosphere is built into the city's oldest tavern, Café Vlissinghe, Blekersstraat 2 (www.cafevlissinghe.be), which dates from 1515. At De Versteende Nacht, Langestraat 11 (tel: 050-33 36 66), you can have a meal and a drink, read comic books (or look at them – they're in Dutch) and listen to jazz from Bebop to modern. The ancient De Garre, just off the Burg at De Garre 1 (www.degarre.be), appeals to those in search of a little authentic atmosphere, while Delaney's at Burg 8 (www.delaneys.be) is an Irish bar-restaurant that has regular evenings of Irish music.

Cycling in Bruges

SPORTS

Switch on any hotel television and you will soon learn that football (soccer) is Belgium's top spectator sport. Bruges has its own football team, Club Brugge KV (www.clubbrugge.be), which is often a challenger for national and European honours, and plays its home games at the Jan Breydelstadion in the Sint-Andries district, to the west of the historic centre of the city. It shares the stadium with the enthusiastic, but far less successful, local side Cercle Brugge (www.cerclebrugge.be).

Cycling is also popular here, and when you are in Bruges, you can obtain information about all aspects of sport and recreation from Sportdienst Brugge (www.brugge.be/vrije-tijd/sport). Many sports facilities are in the suburbs, but are easily reached from the city centre. In Bruges, there are swimming pools in Sint-Kruis and Sint-Andries; in Ghent, the Centre Blaarmeersen offers swimming, squash, tennis and athletics.

ACTIVITIES FOR CHILDREN

Amusement parks. Boudewijn Seapark at A. De Baeckestraat 12 (www.boudewijnseapark.be), includes fairground rides, and Bobo's Indoor, a play area. De Toverplaneet at Legeweg 88 (www.detover-planeet.be) is an indoor playground that is open Wednesdays,

Fridays, weekends and public holidays. In Zeebrugge, a harbour-side theme park called **Seafront Zeebrugge** at Vismijnstraat 7 (www.seafront.be) is usually a winner.

Boats and trams. You can jump on a canal boat from just about anywhere in Bruges or Ghent, and you'll easily entertain the little ones. Trams are equally exciting for kids.

Museums and attractions. Most museums in Bruges will only appeal to older children, but there are some exceptions.

Puppet theatre. In the second half of July Ghent hosts a Puppet Festival (www.puppetbuskersfestival.eu), with stages dotted around town, which is bound to appeal to younger children.

Tours. Horse-drawn carriage rides are popular with children, and you can rent bicycles of sizes to suit the whole family and explore at an appropriate pace.

Old belfry bells in Bruges' Sound Factory

CALENDAR OF EVENTS

For the most up-to-date information and for specific dates on the festivals and arts calendar in Bruges, consult the tourist office (www.visit-bruges.be). The following list gives an idea of some of the major events taking place throughout the year.

April *Bruges:* Cinema Novo Film Festival, held at various venues across the city.

May *Bruges:* Heilig-Bloedprocessie – one of Belgium's most important historical and religious pageants. The Dwars door Brugge road race is also held in May.

Ypres: Kattenstoet (Festival of the Cats) – a colourful medieval pageant that features cats (toy cats!) being thrown from the Belfry by the town jester; takes place every three years (next due in 2024).

July *Bruges:* Festival of Flanders (www.gentfestival.be) – a major festival of classical music that takes place over several months throughout Flanders; venues in Bruges include concert halls, churches and historic buildings; Cactus Festival – celebrating world music at Minnewater.

Ghent: Gentse Feesten – a range of musical and cultural festivities take place in the city centre in a massive 10-day street festival.

August *Bruges:* Early Music Festival, various venues. Pageant of the Golden Tree – commemoration once every five years of the wedding of Charles the Bold and Margaret of York (next due in 2027).

Ghent: Patershol Feesten – various festivities in the Patershol area of the city. International Chamber Music Festival at various venues.

Zeebrugge: Sand Sculpture Festival – stunning transformation of part of the Zeebrugge seashore into towering works of art.

August–September *Bruges:* Zandfeesten, the largest flea market in Flanders (held on Sundays on 't Zand).

October *Ghent:* International Film Festival.

November *Ghent*: legendary Six Days of Ghent cycling event in Het Kuipke stadium.

December *Bruges:* Kerstmarkten – Christmas market and ice-rink on the Markt. *Ghent:* Christmas market at Sint-Baafsplein.

FOOD AND DRINK

Belgians take their eating very seriously. Their rich cuisine and, of course, the *frieten* are world famous. The quality is almost always excellent. Portions are generous; even if you ask for a sandwich, your plate will generally arrive loaded with much more than just garnish. Regional cuisines are strongly defined, but in the cities you should have no trouble sampling dishes from all over Belgium (and beyond).

RESTAURANTS AND BARS

Bruges and Ghent have a great many restaurants, cafés and bars from which to choose. 'Restaurant' can mean anything from a for-mal, top-class establishment to a small and very casual café. Bars can often serve simple, hearty food at fairly reasonable prices. Even in the smallest place you will be served at your table so, if in doubt, simply take your seat and wait for someone to come over: most waiters speak English more or less fluently.

Menus are almost always printed in a variety of languages, and at lunch (*middagmaal*) and dinner (*avondeten*) there is often a choice of set menus at fixed

Mussels, French fries and a local beer are a favourite meal

Bruges' dining scene caters to every taste

prices; these are the best value. Most restaurants also offer a good-value dish of the day *(dagschotel)*. Bars and cafés usually serve snacks in the morning, then lunch from around noon; times and menus are posted in the windows. Many bars stay open until the early hours.

BREAKFAST

Some hotels serve substantial buffet breakfasts *(ontbijt),* which can see you through until lunch time with no trouble at all, though it sometimes costs extra. Along with tea or coffee and fruit juice, there will be a variety of breads, cheeses and cold meats, plus fresh fruit and cereal, yogurt and fruit salads, buns and pastries. You may be asked if you would like a boiled egg, and some of the larger hotels also provide buffet grills, so you can have a fried breakfast as well. Even in the smaller hotels the choice and quality is reasonably good.

COLD DISHES

A *boterham* is an open sandwich, which you will find served just about everywhere. Usually comprising two or three slices of bread with the filling of your choice plus a salad, they are excellent when accompanied by a Belgian beer – and offer great value. There is an enormous range, from salmon to meat to cheeses.

FISH AND SHELLFISH

The close proximity of the North Sea means that fish dominates many menus. Alas, the canals of Bruges and Ghent are now virtually lifeless, but freshwater fish are brought to the table from further afield.

One great favourite is fresh mussels *(mosselen)* in season (from Zeeland, in Holland), which are advertised everywhere when they are available, generally between mid-July and mid-February. Served simply with wedges of lemon, or cooked in a cream, white wine, or garlic and parsley sauce, they are a great delicacy and usually arrive in a large pan from which diners help themselves. Mussels are best eaten with that other great Belgian staple, *frieten* (French fries).

Trout *(forel)* is another firm favourite, often served in a sauce of white wine, and eel *(paling)* crops up on menus a lot, frequently in thick sauces with herbs: *paling in 't groen* – green eel cooked with green herbs – is a speciality, as is *tomates-crevettes* – fresh tomatoes filled with *grijze gaarnalen* (grey shrimp) in Marie Rose sauce. Fresh sole *(zeetong)* is mostly served

Extras

Value-added tax (BTW) is nearly always included in the bill (as is service charge), so there is usually no need to tip unless you want to. However, it is customary to leave at least the small change.

grilled, while oysters, lobsters and crab are dressed in a variety of sauces. Many restaurants have a tank of lobsters or crabs on view to entice customers and prove the freshness of the produce.

The local coastline delivers other types of seafood, such as herring *(haring)*, mostly from Nieuwpoort, which may be lightly salted on the boat and eaten raw as *maatjes*. Herring are also popular – and delicious – when served smoked, steamed, marinated, or in a rich, red wine sauce *(bonne femme)*.

Fish can also feature in the traditional *waterzooi*, a delicately flavoured stew made with vegetables and fish (or sometimes chicken). *Waterzooi op Gentse wijze*, a dish originating from Ghent, is always made with fish.

MEAT AND POULTRY

Game, pork and beef play a prominent part in the Flemish diet, alongside a variety of chicken dishes. *Stoofvlees* is a classic Belgian dish of beef casseroled in beer, with onions and herbs. There are steaks of fine quality, too, usually served with *frieten* (French fries).

You may also come across goose *(gans)*, first boiled and then roasted. Veal *(kalf)* and liver *(lever)* dishes are also widely available. During the game season, rabbit or hare cooked in Gueuze beer with onions and prunes *(konijn met pruimen)* appear on many menus, as well as rich pheasant dishes in thick sauces. *Everzwijn* is wild boar, which comes from the Ardennes, and has lots of flavour.

VEGETABLES AND SALADS

You will find *witloof* (chicory) on most menus, served in a ham and cheese sauce; *stoemp*, a mixture of mashed potatoes and other vegetables, is often served with sausages.

Salad *(sla, salade)* is very much an incidental on Belgian menus, where meat and fish rule supreme. Salads to look out for include the *liégoise*, which contains green beans and potatoes and is served luke-warm, and the *wallonie*, which features a combination of potatoes and bacon.

CHEESE

Cheese *(kaas)* comes in an enormous number of different types, most of them Belgian, Dutch or French. Belgium alone produces 300, including Trappist cheeses such as Orval and Chimay. Belgian Gouda and Remoudou are some of the better-known names. Meals traditionally end with cheese, so leave some room.

DESSERTS AND PÂTISSERIES

The Belgians love a good dessert, and the more chocolate and cream it has the better. *Ijs* (ice cream) and *slagroom* (whipped cream) are usually involved somewhere, perhaps oozing from pancakes or waffles. The ideal way to round off a meal of mussels and chips is with a *dame blanche* –vanilla ice cream and rich, hot chocolate sauce. The selection of cakes, fruit tarts, pastries, buns and biscuits available is immense.

Belgian Blue cattle produce quality beef

SNACKS

French fries are the staple snack of both Bruges and Ghent, sold from stalls and vans dotted around the streets. They can be topped with a variety of calorie-laden sauces: ketchup, mayonnaise, curry – you name it. There are fast-food places all over the towns; in Bruges, they are found mostly around the Markt, 't Zand and Steenstraat, and in Ghent you will see them in Vrijdagmarkt and the Veldstraat area.

Bars generally serve light snacks such as *Croque Monsieur* (toasted ham and cheese sandwich), plus filled rolls *(belegde broodje)*. Sweeter options include the doughy Liège and crispy Brussels waffles.

VEGETARIANS AND VEGANS

Although the Belgian diet is dominated by fish and meat, it is not difficult to adhere to a varied vegetarian regime in Bruges and Ghent. However, this usually means foregoing traditional Flemish cooking. Listed in the Recommended Restaurants section are

Belgian waffles

a number of places that serve vegetarian food. Be careful when ordering not to confuse vegetarian with *vleesgerecht*, which is a meat dish, and to remember also that the Belgian French fry *(friet)* is likely to have been cooked in animal fat. Some 'vegetarian' restaurants also serve meat and fish. If you cannot find a specialist establishment, head for one of the many Italian restaurants – non-meat pasta dishes and salads are usually offered as a matter of course.

DRINKS

Coffee *(koffie)* is fairly strong and usually served with extras such as little biscuits or chocolates, plus two or three kinds of sugar. Coffee liqueurs (especially Irish coffee) are popular and available everywhere. Tea *(thee)* is often served in a glass with lemon and without milk. Lipton-brand herbal teas are also widely available.

Some of Belgium's many varieties of beer *(bier)* are described on page 100. Most bars stock at least 20 or 30, and a few will have more than 100. Those on tap *(van 't vat)* are cheaper than the bottled kind. All the usual spirits are available in generous measures. *Jenever* is the indigenous gin, and it is very strong. Most of the wine *(wijn)* is imported from France and Germany.

Essential bars to visit in Bruges are: 't Brugs Beertje at Kemelstraat 5, where the friendly and knowledgeable landlord will advise you on all aspects of his 300 or so beers; and De Garre, in the alley of the same name off Breidelstraat, which has a comfortable atmosphere and an impressive range of beers that includes its own brand. In Ghent, try Het Waterhuis aan de Bierkant, Groentenmarkt 9, a popular canalside bar with more than 100 beers on offer; Het Spijker (www.hetspijker.be), Pensmarkt 3–5, an underground 13th-century former leprosy shelter; and De Dulle Griet (www.dullegriet.be), Vrijdagmarkt 50, which has more than 250 types of beer, plus 1.5-litre (2.5-pint) elongated Kwak glasses on proud display.

BELGIAN BEERS

Beer is to the Belgians what wine is to the French and, indeed, many Belgian beers complete the last stage of their fermentation in corked bottles. Several hundred different sorts are produced, each of which have their distinctive character – and are served in their own type of glass.

Lambic beers are wild beers, so called because their fermentation involves exposure to the particular wild yeasts prevalent in and around Brussels. Many of these beers have a sour, apple-like taste, but these may have added fruit to impart a distinctive flavour. *Kriek*, a delicious cherry beer, comes in a round glass, while *Frambozen* beer is a pale pink raspberry brew served in a tall-stemmed glass. White beers like the popular Hoegaarden are cloudy and generally light and youthful in flavour.

The label *Trappist* only refers to specialist beers brewed in monasteries. *Tripel* denotes a very strong beer that was served to the abbot and other important personages; the monks drank the *Dubbel*, while the peasants (ie everyone else) had only a watery version.

Kwak (a strong, light-coloured beer) is served in a special glass with a spherical base that sits in a wooden stand in order to remain upright. The 1.5-litre (2.5-pint) glasses and stands are so valuable that customers must often give up a shoe to ensure they don't run off with them.

One of the strongest beers is the appropriately named *Delirium Tremens*, which can take you by surprise if you are not used to it – though if you see pink elephants, they are on the label and not in your head! Another powerful, but delicious, beer is *Corsendonck Agnus Dei*.

Gueuze is a very quaffable, honey-coloured, sour beer served in a straight glass; *Loburg*, a light-coloured beer served in a tall vase-like glass; *Hoegaarden Grand Cru*, a refreshing, coriander-based beer; *Rodenbach Grand Cru*, a red beer with a sharp rusty taste; and *Bourgogne des Flandres*, a light, flavourful red beer.

TO HELP YOU ORDER
I'd like a/an/some… **Heeft u…**

beer bier
bread brood
coffee koffie
dessert nagerecht
fish vis
ice cream ijs
meat vleesgerecht
milk melk
pepper peper

potatoes aardappelen
salad sla, salade
salt zout
soup soep
sugar suiker
tea thee
vegetables groenten
water water
wine wijn

MENU READER
aardbei strawberry
appel apple
bonen beans
boter butter
eend duck
ei egg
garnalen prawns
ham ham
haring herring
honing honey
kaas cheese
kers cherry
kip chicken
koek cake
kool cabbage
kreeft lobster
lam lamb
macaroni noodles

mosselen mussels
nieren kidneys
oesters oysters
peer pear
perzik peach
pruim plum
ree venison
rijst rice
rode wijn red wine
rodekool red cabbage
rund beef
sinaasappel orange
snoek pike
taart flan
varken pork
witte wijn white wine
worst sausage
zalm salmon

WHERE TO EAT

Prices are for a two-course meal including tax but not drinks (or the equivalent). The restaurants listed here accept all major credit cards unless otherwise stated.

€€€€	above 85 euros
€€€	50–85 euros
€€	25–50 euros
€	below 25 euros

BRUGES

Assiette Blanche €€€ *Philipstockstraat 23;* www.assietteblanche.be. Slick and smart French restaurant decorated in a traditional – and very comforting – style. An enterprising menu features such pleasures as lamb couscous and cod fillet in a white wine sauce with mange tout. The main deal here is the set menu.

Bistro Bruut €€€€ *Meestraat 9;* www.bistrobruut.be. Head down a narrow, ancient side street close to the Burg and you'll find this tastefully decorated bistro with a retro feel – love that black and white chequerboard floor. The chef chooses the menu – you just choose the number of courses you want, up to a maximum of five or six. Try, for example, the lobster tartare with Brussels sprouts.

Blackbird € *Jan van Eyckplein 7;* www.blackbird-bruges.com. Cosey spot serving up healthy breakfasts to a trendy crowd. Go for the Piña Colada Smoothie Bowl or a set breakfast with all the trimmings, and you'll be set up for the day. It can be busy, so worth booking ahead.

Breydel-De Coninc €€ *Breidelstraat 24;* www.restaurant-breydel.be. Conveniently located between the Burg and the Markt, this long-standing proponent of the Belgian obsession with mussels has traditional style and wood-beamed ceilings. It serves the mollusc in a variety of ways – the most popular of which is the basic big steaming potful – and all are worth going back for. Other seafood dishes, such as lobster and eels, have a place on the menu too.

Brugs Pitta Huis €€ *Philipstockstraat 35; tel: 050 67 76 11*. This Mediterranean bar offers a nice selection of vegetarian and meat dishes including vegetarian lasagne, falafels, lamb and chicken gyros accompanied by a variety of sauces. Prices are reasonable, though service may be patchy.

De Koetse €€ *Oude Burg 31;* www.dekoetsebrugge.be. Inviting restaurant, just off Simon Stevinplein, with a rustic Flemish interior and a blazing fire in winter. It serves robust Flemish cooking, including spare ribs.

Den Amand €€ *St-Amandsstraat 4;* www.denamand.be. Decorated in pleasant modern style, this small and informal, family-run restaurant offers an inventive range of dishes combining Flemish, Italian and even Asian cuisines.

Den Gouden Karpel €€€ *Vismarkt 9;* www.dengoudenkarpel.be. Where better than a fish market to try great-quality seafood? Expect expert renderings of classic fish dishes: from bouillabaisse to bisque.

De Schaar €€€ *Hooistraat 2;* www.bistrodeschaar.be. This appealing restaurant sits prettily beside the Coupure canal about ten minutes' walk southeast of the Burg. The speciality here is grilled meat – for example rack of lamb with wok vegetables and mustard sauce – but there are other gastronomic delights too, for instance duck with a raspberry sauce. All are nicely served and presented.

De Stove €€ *Kleine Sint-Amandsstraat 4;* www.restaurantdestove.be. An intimate restaurant with a 20-year reputation, just west of the Markt. Family-owned and operated, it specialises in Flemish dishes, with an emphasis on salads, fish and steaks.

Diligence €€ *Hoogstraat 5;* www.diligence-brugge.be. In a great location, in an old and attractive building metres from the Burg, this popular restaurant does a tasty line in traditional Flemish dishes – try the mussels and chips, for example. Film buffs will want to know that a scene of In Bruges was shot here.

Duc de Bourgogne €€€ *Huidenvettersplein 12;* www.ducdebourgogne.be. A classic Bruges dining experience. Serves French dishes in baronial surroundings, with a canal view that is one of the city's most photographed.

Goesepitte 43 €€€ *Goezeputstraat 43;* www.goesepitte43.be.The contemporary décor here is inventive and creative – there's even a moss wall made up of real moss at the entrance - and so is the menu: try, for example, the guinea fowl filet filled with goose liver as a main. After the kitchen closes, the place morphs into a relaxed and really rather charming bar.

Het Mozarthuys €€ *Huidenvettersplein 1;* www.mozarthuys.com. Guess which famous composer's music wafts among the tables at this old-style Flemish restaurant? Yes, you can hum along to Wolfgang Amadeus while you enjoy its speciality grilled meat dishes and mussels. Lovely if very busy outdoor terrace in good weather.

Huidevettershuis €€ *Huidenvettersplein 10;* www.huidevettershuis.be. An elegant canal-side eatery (the entrance is just off Vismarkt), specialising in Flemish cuisine. The building, which was formerly the Tanners' Guild House, dates from 1630.

Le Pain Quotidien € Simon Stevinplein 15; www.lepainquotidien.com. Fresh breads and cakes are on sale here. Go for breakfast, lunch or tea to revel in the family atmosphere. A large central table dominates the room and there's a garden terrace out back.

Maximiliaan van Oostenrijk €€ *Wijngaardplein 16–17;* www.maximiliaan-vanoostenrijk.be. Burgundian restaurant in one of the most romantic parts of the city, adjacent to the Begijnhof. Specialities include the traditional local stew, *waterzooï*, grilled meats and seafood.

Patrick Devos €€€€ *Zilverstraat 41;* www.patrickdevos.be. Lavishly appointed restaurant, set in a 13th-century building that serves as a showplace for chef/owner Patrick Devos' stunning creations using fresh regional produce wherever feasible.

Pietje Pek €€ *Sint-Jakobsstraat 13;* www.pietjepek.com. Behind its notable Art Nouveau façade, this restaurant serves satisfying portions of its speciality cheese and meat fondues, as well as an all-you-can-eat menu.

't Bourgondisch Cruyce €€€€ *Wollestraat 41–3;* www.relaisbourgondisch cruyce.be. This is generally regarded as one of the best, most atmospheric dining experiences in Bruges, set in a beautiful old hotel overlooking the canal, serving Flemish regional specialities.

Tom Pouce €€ *Burg 17;* www.tompoucebrugge.be. This is a large restaurant, but it manages not to be impersonal, and it enjoys an unrivalled position on the Burg. Although fish and Flemish cuisine dominate the menu, the quality of the food is secondary to that of the location. Order a waffle or pancake, sit on the heated outdoor terrace and watch the world go by.

Zet'Joe €€€€ *Langestraat 11;* www.zetjoe.be/en. Indefatigable owner-chef Geert Van Hecke has created this recently opened restaurant after closure of the legendary De Karmeliet, which used to be just a few buildings up on the same street. Despite its ordinary name, the restaurant occupies a gastronomic class of its own. Beautiful interior is accompanied by excellent, though not cheap, haute cuisine. Set menus are the order of the day.

GHENT

Brasserie HA' €€€ *Kouter 29;* www.brasserieha.be. Elegant yet cool, the theatre's café-restaurant serves refined French and Belgian cuisine – light and breezy for lunch, candle-lit romantic for dinner. A multi-coloured modern chandelier graces the main dining room, and in the summer you can enjoy your meal seated on the lovely outside terrace overlooking the Ketelvaart canal.

Chubby Cheeks €€€ *Onderbergen 33;* www.chubbycheeks.be. This fabulous restaurant is food as an adventure with an ingenious menu featuring tapas-style dishes like swiss chard and beetroot. There is an open kitchen – so perch on a stool and watch – or opt for one of a handful of tables.

Keizershof €€ *Vrijdagmarkt 47;* www.keizershof.net. This large, rambling restaurant has so much space that even when it's full it won't seem crowded. Diners pile into hearty portions of Belgian and continental food, amid decor that features wooden ceiling beams, plain wood tables and fashionably unadorned walls. In summer, there are outdoor tables in the courtyard.

La Malcontenta €€ *Haringsteeg 7–9;* www.lamalcontenta.be. This Patershol-district restaurant serves one of the most specific of specialities – cuisine from the Canary Islands. This means plenty of fish, paella, *patatas arrugadas* (tiny new potatoes cooked in their skins in very salty water) and *mojo* sauce (made with olive oil, vinegar, garlic and coriander).

Pakhuis €€ *Schuurkenstraat 4;* www.pakhuis.be. Pakhuis is a lively brasserie south of Sint-Niklaaskerk, offering good modern Flemish and Franco-Italian cuisine. Its setting inside a restored former warehouse is especially impressive. Oyster and seafood platters are the speciality of the house.

Patiron € *Sluizeken 30;* www.patiron.be. A delightful bio café north of the city centre, where everything is made on the premises, including some hearty soups. The main speciality, however, is quiche, with more than 80 delicious varieties to choose from.

't Klaverblad €€€ *Corduwanierstraat 61;* www.restoklaverblad.be. While most of the neighbouring restaurants in the Patershol try to lure you with music, 'themed cuisine' and moderate prices, 't Klaverblad is unashamedly gastronomic and expensive. French food is prepared with a Flemish twist, for serious eaters who appreciate good food.

Vier Tafels €€ *Plotersgracht 6;* www.restaurantviertafels.be/english. Located on one of the narrow alleys of the Patershol district, this restaurant started with just four tables, hence its name. Now considerably enlarged, it has an adventurous menu of dishes from around the world.

TRAVEL ESSENTIALS

PRACTICAL INFORMATION

A Accessible Travel 108
Accommodation 108
Airport 109
B Bicycle rental 110
Budgeting for
  your trip 110
C Camping 111
Car hire 112
Climate 112
Clothing 113
Crime and safety 113
D Driving 113
E Electricity 115
Embassies and
  consulates 115
Emergencies 115
G Getting there 116
Guides and tours 117
H Health and
  medical care 118

L Language 118
LGBTQ+ travellers 120
M Maps 120
Media 120
Money 120
O Opening times 121
P Police 122
Post offices 122
Public holidays 122
R Religion 123
T Telephones 123
Time zones 124
Tipping 125
Toilets 125
Tourist information 125
Transport 125
V Visas and entry
  requirements 126
W Websites 127
Y Youth hostels 127

A

ACCESSIBLE TRAVEL

Facilities, accessibility to transport, and buildings in both cities are distinctly patchy. The cobblestone streets and medieval buildings of Bruges mean access to some places of interest can be challenging, particularly as ramps and railings are invariably absent. Some hotels have ramps, but planning rules for older hotels forbid the installation of lifts (elevators), so some or all of the rooms can only be reached by the staircase. Museums are often similarly restricted, and may involve numerous stairs. Detailed information is available online at www.visitbruges.be.

Some of the larger (chain) hotels have specially designed rooms for guests with disabilities. There are, at most, usually two or three such rooms per hotel.

The new De Lijn buses are equipped with a low floor, ramp and hydraulic lifting device. They provide marked places reserved for disabled passengers, which are at the front of the bus by at the wheelchair accessible door. More details can be found on the De Lijn website: www.delijn.be/en. At some major road crossings in both cities, textured soft paving has been installed. All travellers should be careful near the canals, which often are not railed off from the footpath or road.

Bruges tourist information office produces a map showing free parking facilities for drivers with disabilities. Access Info (tel: 070 23 30 50; www.access-info.be), a branch of the Flemish Tourist Board, also has updates on disabled access. In the UK, information may be obtained from Tourism for All (www.tourismforall.org.uk).

In the US, contact the Society for the Advancement of Travel for the Handicapped (sath), www.sath.org.

ACCOMMODATION (see also Camping, Youth hostels, and the Recommended hotels chapter)

Bruges is particularly busy in the summer months, at Easter and at weekends, so it is advisable to book well in advance if you plan to visit at these times. If you are travelling in the low season or during the week, ask about discounts – many hotels do special deals from about October to March. The rates on page 128 we have given are averages for double rooms in high season. Service charges and taxes are included. There is often a supplement for single rooms.

There is a star rating system (indicated in the tourist information literature and by the front door of the hotel), but the number of stars bears little relation to what you may get. Some four-star hotels may have certain facilities but not be very pleasant, while hotels further down the scale can be delightful. A few hotel exteriors and foyers look splendid, but this can be deceptive. Inspect rooms first if you can.

A substantial breakfast is sometimes included in the hotel rate, but often-times hotels charge extra. This can add considerably to the price, so it may be worth looking for a local café that serves a good breakfast. The Bruges tourist office also supplies a list of bed-and-breakfast accommodation on its website (www.visitbtruges.be).

The tourist offices in Bruges and Ghent can provide detailed lists of hotels in each city that describe facilities, prices and contact detail. You can also find them at Bruges official tourist website, www.visitbruges.be.

Please note that the city of Bruges charges a €4 tourism tax per person (over 18) per night.

How much per night/week? **Hoeveel kost het per nacht/week?**

AIRPORT

Brussels Airport (BRU) (www.brusselsairport.be) is located in Zaventem, 13km (9 miles) from the centre of the capital and served by most major air-lines. It has all the facilities you would expect of an international airport.

There are train, bus and taxi connections from the airport to Brussels – the train links are the most efficient, running every 15 minutes at peak times from the airport to all three of Brussels' main stations. From these there are regular train links to Bruges and Ghent; the travel time from Brussels is about an hour to Bruges and 30 minutes to Ghent.

The trip by taxi from the airport to the centre of Brussels will cost you substantially more than the train, but a reduction in the taxi fare is available if you present a round-trip air ticket.

B

BICYCLE RENTAL

Bruges encourages cyclists by allowing them to travel down more than 50 one-way streets in either direction. It's not as dangerous as it sounds, due to the special cycle lanes. The Bruges tourist office and website has a full list of which establishments rent bikes. Some hotels put bikes at their guests' disposal; ask when you arrive. They can be hired from the railway station in Bruges and other towns by the day. A discount is offered if you present a valid train ticket. Bikes can be left at other participating rail stations – an information leaflet is available from stations. Among other hire locations in Bruges are Hotel Koffieboontje at Hallestraat 4 (tel: 050-33 80 27), Fietsen Popelier at Mariastraat 26 (tel: 050-34 32 62), and Bruges Bike Rental at Niklaas Desparsstraat 17 (www.brugesbikerental.be).

I'd like to hire a bicycle **Ik wil graag een fiets huren**

BUDGETING FOR YOUR TRIP

Bruges can be expensive, but no more so than other popular European tourist destinations, and less so in many respects than Belgium's capital, Brussels.
Getting to Belgium. The cost of getting to Belgium from the UK and Ireland by air varies considerably. Flying with Ryanair one way from various airports in both countries to Brussels-Charleroi Airport can cost only a few pounds or euros (plus taxes and other charges), but £80 (€95) one way is probably nearer the average, and can easily go higher. These rates have forced carriers such as BA, BMI, Aer Lingus and Brussels Airlines to cut their fares for flights

into Brussels Airport.

Of the other options, going by bus from London to Bruges is likely to be the cheapest. By train, Eurostar from London St Pancras Station to Brussels offers discounted advance-purchase tickets, as does the Channel Tunnel car-transporter.

Accommodation. For a double room with en-suite bathroom and breakfast in Bruges you can pay around €100, but for reasonable comfort and facilities, €130 is a more realistic starting point; a mid-range hotel will cost €150–250; and expensive hotels begin at about €250. What you get obviously varies with the location and the time of year. At the busiest times – and Bruges is very often busy – rooms can be hard to come by.

Eating out. You can eat well in many of Bruges' restaurants for about €40 per person for a three-course meal without wine. However, a more realistic starting point would be €60; in mid-range establishments, expect to pay €75; and in an expensive restaurant, more than €75. If you are on a tight budget look for the *dagschotel* (dish of the day) or the *dagmenu* (menu of the day), available in some restaurants, which will offer a worthwhile saving. Alternatively, eat in a café (bar) that serves low-cost food – this could be a simple spaghetti bolognese or *biefstuk met frieten/steak-friet* (steak and fries).

Museums. Public museums charge in the region of €15 for adult admission, while privately owned attractions may cost up to €20; you might be able to save money by buying a Museum Card (see page 25). There are reduced rates for children, senior citizens and students.

Public transport. A single ticket covering the city costs €2.50; it is valid for 60 minutes. A one-day pass (dagpas) costs €7.50; multi-day passes are available. For details see www.delijn.be.

C

CAMPING

Belgium's campsites are graded from one to four stars and are usually excellently equipped. There is just one campsite in Bruges that is close enough to permit easy use of public transport into the city centre, though there are others farther away, and along the Belgian coast. The all-year Camping Memling (Veltemweg 109, 8310 Bruges; tel: 050-35 58 45; www.camping-memling.be) is in the Sint-Kruis district in the east of the city. It is advisable to book pitches in advance during the high season. Spending the night in cars, caravans, mobile homes or tents by the roadside, in woods, dunes or directly on the beach is forbidden.

CAR HIRE (see also Driving)

With a city centre as compact as that of Bruges, a well-organised public transport bus system, and strict rules regulating parking, there is no need for a car in the city. If you want to explore the countryside around Bruges, to include the nearby coast and World War I battlefields around Ieper (Ypres), you may want to hire a car for a day or two. Major car hire firms are represented in the city and are listed on www.visitbruges.be. If time permits you should compare prices.

The minimum age to hire a car may be 21 or 25, depending on the company and the vehicle. Credit cards are almost always required for payment, and you will need to show your (clean) driving licence and passport.

Many hotels have arrangements with car hire companies that make it simple to arrange for a car, but a small extra charge will normally be made for delivery to your hotel.

CLIMATE

Belgium has a temperate climate much influenced by its proximity to the sea, although obviously this influence diminishes inland. The warmest and driest weather is between April and October, but it can rain at any time of the year. Approximate monthly temperatures in Bruges are shown below. You can obtain a current weather forecast at www.meteo.be.

	J	F	M	A	M	J	J	A	S	O	N	D
°C	5	6	10	13	19	21	23	22	20	14	8	6
°F	41	43	50	55	66	70	74	72	68	57	46	41

CLOTHING

The unpredictable climate means you should be prepared for rain at any time of the year. A raincoat is advisable, although many upmarket hotels provide complimentary umbrellas. In March and April, the weather can be bright and reasonably warm, but with sudden blasts of cold wind as you turn a corner; so a light coat that can be slipped on and off is a good idea. In winter, heavy coats and sweaters are advisable. Bruges is a walking city, so take comfortable, reliable shoes that you know will not hurt your feet, and take care on the cobblestones.

Dress is generally smart but relaxed and informal.

CRIME AND SAFETY (see also Police)

Its compactness and the numbers of tourists wandering its streets make Bruges extremely safe: you are seldom alone or far from the centre. There is very little crime, though obviously it makes sense to take elementary precautions with cameras, bags and personal effects. Valuables should be left in your hotel safe.

Ghent is very safe, too, but it is wise to stay alert in the area around Sint-Pietersstation late at night.

D

DRIVING (see also Car hire)

To take your car into Belgium, you will need:

International driving licence or your own national licence (held for at least a year).

Car registration papers.

Green Card (this does not provide cover, but is internationally recognised proof that you have insurance – not obligatory for EU countries).

Fire extinguisher, red warning triangle and reflective jacket in case of breakdown.

National identity sticker for your car, or an EU licence plate.

Headlight adaptors for right-hand-drive vehicles, to prevent the lights dazzling oncoming drivers.

Warning triangle and reflective vest.

Driving conditions. Drive on the right, pass on the left. Though you may wish to drive to and from Bruges, it is unnecessary and ill-advised to drive within the city itself. Bruges has a complex one-way system, with narrow winding roads that in high season are clogged with pedestrians, bicycles and horse-drawn carriages. Driving in Ghent is more aggressive than in Bruges and is made more complicated by the presence of trams, which you are not allowed to overtake and to which you must give way.

Belgium's motorway system is excellent, but it and the city ring-roads (like that in Bruges) can get clogged at rush hour. Other main roads in Flanders are generally very straight and free of traffic.

Rules of the road. Seat belts must be worn by both driver and passengers and there are stiff penalties for speeding and drink driving. Some offences require payment of fines on the spot.

An important rule to remember is that drivers should normally yield to traffic approaching from the right. A yellow diamond-shaped sign with a white border indicates that drivers on main roads have the right of way. When the sign reappears with a diagonal line through it, then drivers must yield to traffic from the right.

Speed limits. On motorways, the limit is 120km/h (75mph) and on other main roads it is 90km/h (55mph) in Wallonia and Brussels, and 70km/h (44mph) in Flanders. In residential areas the speed limit drops to 50km/h (30mph) or even 30km/h (18mph).

Parking. There is limited parking in the city centres. Larger car and coach parks exist around the perimeter of Bruges and on the edge of Ghent's pedestrian zone; it is safer (and quicker) to use them and walk into the centre. Both tourist offices provide maps indicating car parks.

Breakdown. Belgium's two main motoring organisations are the Touring Club de Belgique (www.touring.be) and the Royal Automobile Club de Belgique (www.racb.com). They have reciprocal arrangements with other national motoring organisations. Motorways have emergency phones positioned at regular intervals.

Fuel and oil. Service stations are plentiful, and most international brands of unleaded (*loodvrij*) petrol (gasoline) and diesel are on sale. Electric charging points are on the increase.

Road signs. International pictographs are widely used, but here are some written signs you may encounter:

rechtdoor straight ahead
links left
rechts right
op/om de hoek on/around the corner
bij het stoplicht at the traffic light
voorrang verlenen yield
benzine gas (petrol)

loodvrij unleaded
normaal regular
Fill it up, please **Vol, alstublieft**
Is this the right road to…? **Is dit de juiste weg naar…?**
I have a puncture/flat tyre **Ik heb een lek/lekke band**
My car broke down **Ik heb autopech**

E

ELECTRICITY
The current is 220 volts AC, with standard European-style two-pin plugs. British equipment needs only a plug adaptor; American apparatus requires a transformer and an adaptor.

EMBASSIES AND CONSULATES
All the foreign embassies and consulates in Belgium are in Brussels. For further information, consult www.diplomatie.belgium.be/en.
Belgian embassies and consulates abroad
Australia www.australia.diplomatie.belgium.be/en
Canada www.canada.diplomatie.belgium.be/en
Ireland www.ireland.diplomatie.belgium.be/en
South Africa www.southafrica.diplomatie.belgium.be/en
UK www.unitedkingdom.diplomatie.belgium.be/en
US www.unitedstates.diplomatie.belgium.be/en

EMERGENCIES (see also Health and Police)
The three-digit emergency telephone numbers listed below are valid

throughout Belgium:
General emergency number: 112
Police assistance: 101

> I need an English-speaking doctor/dentist **Ik zoek een dokter/
> tandarts die Engels spreekt**

G

GETTING THERE

By air. Brussels Airport is linked by direct flights with all European and many North American cities, but other long-distance travellers may have to connect via a hub airport, usually Amsterdam, London or Paris. Brussels Airlines (www.brusselsairlines.com), is the main local carrier. British Airways (www.britishairways.com) flies from several UK airports to Brussels; flight time from London is about one hour. Several other airlines fly from UK airports to Brussels. These include KLM (www.klm.com). Aer Lingus (www.aerlingus.com) has regular service to Brussels from Dublin and Cork. Ryanair (www.ryanair.com) flies from airports in Britain and Ireland to Charleroi, near Brussels.

By rail. Brussels and Bruges have excellent rail connections with the rest of the European network. There are various deals and discounts, and it is best to contact your local rail operator for the latest information before your trip.

From the UK it is possible to reach Bruges and Ghent easily via the Eurostar service through the Channel Tunnel to Brussels. Trains depart from St Pancras International in London and arrive in Brussels within one hour 50 minutes. You can be in Bruges or Ghent in just over three hours. Allow time for going through customs at St Pancras. Trains start boarding 20 minutes before they leave. Your bags stay with you at all times, so there is no delay waiting for luggage once you arrive. Trains are comfortable, and there is a café/bar on board.

Seats can be chosen and reserved when booking your ticket online (www.eurostar.com), or at some mainline stations and travel agents.

If you want to take your car, Eurotunnel (www.eurotunnel.com) trains travel via the Channel Tunnel between Folkestone and Calais every 15 minutes. Passengers stay with their car for the 35-minute journey.

By bus. Flixbus (www.flixbus.co.uk) operates bus services between all major European cities and Brussels; those coming from London generally stop in Bruges.

By boat. There are currently no car ferries from the UK to Belgium. The nearest to Bruges you will get is on the Hull to Rotterdam ferry operated by P&O Ferries (www.poferries.com).

GUIDES AND TOURS

Guided tours allow you to explore parts of the city that you might not discover on your own. Groups and individuals can book qualified and very informative guides in advance from the tourist office, for a minimum two-hour tour. For details, see www.visitbruges.be.

Bruges's canals can be explored by boat from 10am–6pm daily March–mid-November. Boats depart from Rozenhoedkaai, Dijver and Mariastraat. Night tours for groups can also be arranged on request, and can be very appealing. It can be chilly on these tour boats, and even on a warm summer day you may be grateful for a sweater or jacket.

A 50-minute tour round Bruges by bus with recorded commentary in the language of your choice serves as a popular introduction to the city – if you can stand the commentary. Tours are operated by City Tour (www.citytour.be), with minibuses departing from the Markt every 30 minutes. Rival operators run two-hour tours to Damme, depending on the season: they also depart from the Markt and can include a free drink and pancake in Damme, and a return canal trip on the Lamme Goedzak paddle-boat (www.lammegoedzakdamme.com).

Quasimodo (www.quasimodo.be) run minibus tours of the country-side and the Flanders Fields battle grounds. Horse-drawn carriage rides through the city centre depart from the Markt (occasionally from the Burg).

Quasimundo (www.quasimundo.eu) – not to be confused with the Quasimodo above – runs cycling tours in and around Bruges. Tours, which last two hours and 30 minutes, include provision of a mountain bike, guide, transport by bus, insurance and rain gear.

H

HEALTH AND MEDICAL CARE (see also Emergencies)

Travellers from EU countries should receive free or discounted medical treatment in Belgium on presentation of a European Health Insurance Card (EHIC). Non-EU citizens need to take out travel insurance, which should cover illness, accident and lost luggage.

A Belgian pharmacy *(apotheek)* is identified by a green cross and should have a list in the window of nearby late-night chemist shops.

For urgent medical treatment, call 112.

Where's the nearest pharmacy (chemist)? **Waar is de dichtstbijzijnde apotheek?**

L

LANGUAGE

In Flanders, which covers roughly the northern half of Belgium, residents speak Flemish (a dialect of Dutch) and this is the language you hear in Bruges and Ghent. French is the language of Wallonia, southern Belgium. Brussels is officially bilingual, but has more French than Dutch speakers. A German-speaking minority of around 70,000 lives in the eastern districts of the country.

English is spoken by many and should be at least partially understood by virtually everybody. Written and spoken Dutch contains many English loan-words and can sound familiar; at other times there are no clues as to meaning. Menus are usually printed in English as well as Dutch and French; if they are not, most members of staff will be happy to explain what things mean.

Although local road signs are in Dutch, be aware that in this bilingual country many towns bear different names in French: Brugge (Dutch) is *Bruges* in French, Gent is *Gand*, Ieper is *Ypres*, Oudenaarde is *Audenarde*, and Antwerpen is *Anvers*.

Hello/hi **Dag/hallo**

Good morning **Goedemorgen**

Good afternoon **Goedemiddag**

Good evening **Goedenavond**

What's your name? **Hoe heet u?**

My name is… **Mijn naam is…**

Goodbye/see you soon
   Dag/tot ziens

Days and Numbers

Yes **Ja**

No **Nee**

I'd like… **Ik wil graag…**

How much? **Hoeveel kost het?**

Where is/are…?
   Waar is/zijn…?

Please **Alstublieft**

Thank you **Dank u wel**

Monday **Maandag**

Tuesday **Dinsdag**

Wednesday **Woensdag**

Thursday **Donderdag**

Friday **Vrijdag**

Saturday **Zaterdag**

Sunday **Zondag**

0 **nul**

1 **één**

2 **twee**

3 **drie**

4 **vier**

5 **vijf**

6 **zes**

7 **zeven**

8 **acht**

9 **negen**

10 **tien**

11 **elf**

12 **twaalf**

13 **dertien**

14 **veertien**

15 **vijftien**

16 **zestien**

17 **zeventien**

18 **achttien**

19 **negentien**

20 **twintig**

Communications

Where's an internet café? **Waar vind ik een internetcafe?**

How much per hour/half hour? **Hoeveel kost het per uur/
   half uur?**

Does it have wireless internet? **Is er draadloos internet?**

What is the WiFi password? **Wat is het wifi wachtwoord?**

Is the WiFi free? **Is wifi gratis?**

Are you on Facebook/Twitter? **Bent u op Facebook/Twitter?**

LGBTQ+ TRAVELLERS

For information on the LGBTQ+ scene in Bruges, Jong & Hib in Brugge (www.j-h.be) is a great place to start. For LGBTQ+-friendly hotels and B&Bs use EBAB (www.ebab.com), a specialist accommodation search engine.

M

MAPS

Bruges' tourist office produces a free comprehensive map of central Bruges, and several commercial maps can be bought at bookshops and newsagents around town.

MEDIA

Newspapers and magazines. English-language publications are sold at station kiosks, larger bookshops and newsstands. Larger hotels may stock the *International Herald Tribune*, *Financial Times* and other international newspapers.

Have you any English newspapers? **Heeft u Engelse kranten?**

Radio and television. BBC long-wave and world services and European-based American networks can be picked up easily. Most hotels have cable television with up to 30 channels, including BBC World News from the UK and CNN International from the US. Many European channels show English-language films (around 9pm) and programmes with subtitles.

MONEY

Currency. The unit of currency in Belgium is the euro, which is abbreviated to € and divided into 100 cents. Coins are: €2, €1, and 50, 20, 10, 5, 2 and 1 cents. Banknotes are in denominations of €500, 200, 100, 50, 20 10 and 5. The €500 and €200 notes are rarely if ever seen in circulation, and some small businesses may be reluctant to accept either.

Exchange facilities. There is a standard commission for changing foreign currency and travellers' cheques. Generally, banks offer the best rates, followed by bureaux de change. Hotels will often exchange currency, but at an inferior rate. Currency-exchange machines at Brussels Airport make transactions in several currencies. ATMs accepting non-Belgian debit and credit cards are widely available.

Credit and debit cards. The vast majority of hotels, restaurants and shops accept payment by international credit and debit cards.

Sales tax, service charge. Called BTW, a sales (value-added) tax is imposed on most goods and services in Belgium. In hotels and most restaurants, this is often accompanied by a service charge. Both charges are included in the bill. To recover some of the tax on expensive purchases, look for shops displaying signs saying 'Europe Tax-Free Shopping' or 'Tax-Free International'; retailers are well acquainted with the necessary procedures.

I'd like to change some dollars/pounds into euros. **Ik wil graag wat dollars/ponden in euro's omwisselen.**
Can I pay by credit card? **Kan ik met een creditcard betalen?**

OPENING TIMES

Banks open Monday–Friday 9am–noon, 2–4pm and some until 5pm. Some banks open on Saturday morning and until 6pm on one or two days a week, check online before heading to a branch.

Shops and department stores are generally open Monday–Saturday 10am–6 or 6.30pm, but Sunday opening is becoming increasingly commonplace.

Museums are generally open Tuesday to Sunday from 9.30 or 10am to 5pm. In Bruges, some may be closed on Tuesday or Wednesday instead of Monday.

P

POLICE (see also Emergencies)

The *politie* or police can be reached on the emergency 101 phone number. They are not that noticeable on the streets (there is seldom any need for them in Bruges), but they are usually dressed in dark blue. Any theft should be reported at the nearest police station. The main police station in Bruges is at Lodewijk Coiseaukaai 3, tel: 050-44 88 44.

Where's the police station? **War is het politiebureau?**

POST OFFICES

Belgium has an efficient postal system with its post boxes painted red. Mail to the US takes seven days or so, within Europe two to three days. Post offices are now thin on the ground, but stamps are sold at a wide range of outlets including many shops and hotels. The main post office in Bruges is well to the west of the city centre at Smedenstraat 57 (Mon–Fri 9am–6pm, Sat 9am–3pm); in Ghent, the main post office is at Lange Kruisstraat 55 (Mon–Fri 9.30am–6pm, Sat 9.30am–3pm).

A stamp for this letter/postcard, please. **Een postzegel voor deze brief/ansichtkaart, alstublieft.**
I want to send this package by airmail/express. **Ik wil dit pakje per luchtpost/expres versturen.**

PUBLIC HOLIDAYS

Most shops and other businesses are closed on public holidays; if museums are not closed, they will be operating on Sunday hours. If a holiday falls on a Sunday, the following Monday will usually be taken off instead.

1 January *Nieuwjaar* New Year's Day
1 May *Dag van de Arbeid* Labour Day
11 July *Feest van de Vlaamse* Flanders Day
21 July *Nationalefeestdag* National Day
15 August *Maria Hemelvaart* Assumption
1 November *Allerheiligen* All Saints' Day
11 November *Wapenstilstand* Armistice Day
25 December *Kerstdag* Christmas Day
Moveable dates:
Pasen Easter
Paasmaandag Easter Monday
Hemelvaartsdag Ascension Day
Pinkstermaandag Whit Monday

R

RELIGION

Belgium's population is predominantly Roman Catholic, but Protestant churches are also well represented in both cities. In Bruges, there is an English-language Anglican service held at Saint Peter's Chapel at Keerstraat 1 most Sundays – for times and further details go to www.visitbruges.be.

T

TELEPHONES

All but the remotest parts of Belgium are on the **mobile phone (cell phone)** network at GSM900/1800, the band common to the rest of Europe, Australia and New Zealand. Mobile/cell phones bought in North America will need to be able to adjust to this GSM band. If you intend to use your own mobile/cell phone in Belgium, you may want to check call rates with your supplier before you depart. You may find it cheaper to buy a **local SIM card**, though this can get complicated: some mobiles/cells will not permit you to swap SIM cards and the connection instructions for the replacement SIM card may not be in English. If you overcome these problems, you can buy local SIM cards at high-street phone companies, which offer myriad deals beginning at about €5 per SIM card.

There are **no area codes**, but Belgian numbers mostly begin with a zero, a relic of former area codes, which have now been incorporated into the numbers themselves. Telephone numbers beginning 0900 or 070 are premium-rated, 0800 are toll-free. There's no distinction between local and long-distance calls – in other words calling Ostend from Bruges costs the same as calling a number in Brussels.

International phone calls

To make an international phone call from Belgium, dial the appropriate international access code as below, then the number you require, omitting the initial zero where there is one.

Australia 0061
Canada 001
Republic of Ireland 00353
New Zealand 0064
South Africa 0027
UK 0044
US 001

Phoning Belgium from abroad

To call Belgium from abroad, dial your international access code, then 32 (the country code for Belgium), followed by the subscriber number minus its initial zero where there is one.

TIME ZONES

The following chart shows the time difference between Belgium and various cities in winter. Between the beginning of April and the end of October, Belgian clocks are put forward one hour.

New York	London	**Belgium**	Jo'burg	Sydney	Auckland
6am	11am	**noon**	1pm	10pm	midnight

TIPPING

In a country where service is included in most bills, tipping is not a problem. Most people will not expect a tip (but will appreciate it if you give them one). Exceptions include public toilets, where the attendant will expect a tip of 35–50 cents, and porter and maid service in the more expensive hotels.

TOILETS

A toilet is generally called a WC (pronounced vay-say) in Flanders. If there is not a graphic of some kind that leaves no room for doubt about which toilet is for females and which for males, look for the words *dames* (women) and *heren* (men). In small cafés and restaurants, men's and women's toilets may be only notionally separated.

TOURIST INFORMATION

The main information office in Bruges is in the Concertgebouw, 't Zand 34 (www.visitbruges.be). There is also a tourist information office in the station, on Stationsplein, as well as at Markt 1 inside the Historium museum (see page 27).

In Ghent, the tourist office is located inside the renovated Oude Vismijn at Sint-Veerleplein 5 (www.visitgent.be).

Where is the tourist office? **Waar is het toeristen-bureau?**

TRANSPORT

In the city, where everything seems to be a short walk away, public transport is not usually a problem.

Buses. In Bruges, buses to the suburbs can be caught most conveniently near the Markt or at the railway station. Sightseeing buses and excursions also depart from the Markt or its immediate vicinity. Other main bus stops are at Dijver, Biekorf and Kuipersstraat. A one-day pass (€7.50) allows unlimited travel on all the city's buses. Regional buses (to destinations outside Bruges) can be caught at the railway station and in 't Zand. These are operated by De

Lijn whose website has an excellent route planner (www.delijn.be).

In Ghent, the main bus station is outside Sint-Pieters railway station. This is also a terminus for many of the city's trams, which serve most of Ghent and are great fun to ride. Buses and trams can also be caught from the city centre, at Korenmarkt. With major stops in Ostend, the coastal tram (www.delijn.be) is an excellent way to explore the Flemish coast.

When's the next bus/train to…? **Wanneer vertrekt de volgende bus/trein naar…?**
I want a ticket to… **Ik wil graag een kaart naar…**
A one-way/return-trip ticket **Enkeltje/retourtje**
A first-class/economy-class ticket **Kaartje eerste klas/tweede klas**

Taxis. Taxis are plentiful in both Bruges and Ghent, where they flock together outside the railway stations for the hotel run. Order your taxi at the hotel when you check out, and one will arrive in two or three minutes. However, taxis are rather more difficult to hail in the streets – in Bruges, you are most likely to find one in the sidestreets off the Markt, while in Ghent the best place to try hailing a taxi is Kouter.

Trains. The Belgian railway network is superb. Bruges and Ghent are situated on the same line that connects Brussels with Ostend. Train services are prompt and frequent. Announcements on inter-city trains are given in Dutch and French, and text-screen panels in each carriage give the name of the next station. Information and assistance are available at both cities' railway stations.

There are first- and second-class carriages. Smoking is banned on all trains. A range of discounts is offered at weekends and on seasonal passes.

V

VISAS AND ENTRY REQUIREMENTS

Citizens of the EU (European Union) and EEA (European Economic Area), plus citizens of the UK, Australia, New Zealand, Canada and the US do not need a visa to enter Belgium if staying for ninety days or less, but they do need a current passport (or EU national identity card), whose validity exceeds the length of their stay by at least three months. Travellers from South Africa, on the other hand, need a passport and a tourist visa for visits of less than ninety days; visas must be obtained before departure and are available from the appropriate embassy (115). For stays of longer than ninety days, EU/EEA residents will have few problems, but everyone else needs a mix of visas and permits. In all cases, consult the appropriate embassy at home before departure.

As Belgium is a member of the European Union (EU), free exchange of non-duty-free goods for personal use is permitted between Belgium and Ireland, but not the UK.

Currency restrictions. There is no limit on the amount of euros or other currency that can be brought into or taken out of the country by residents and non-residents up to €10,000.

WEBSITES

Useful general information can be found at www.visitbelgium.com and www.visitflanders.com. The local tourist boards for both Bruges and Ghent operate easy to navigate websites giving information on hotels, attractions, and more: www.visitbruges.be and www.visitgent.be.

YOUTH HOSTELS

Bruges and its immediate neighbourhood have a number of 'Youth Hotels' and Youth Hostels. There are three located in the city itself, notably:

Bauhaus International Youth & Budget Hotel, Langestraat 133–7, 8000 Bruges, www.bauhaus.be

The Passage, Dweersstraat 26, 8000 Bruges, www.passagebruges.com

Snuffel Backpackers Hostel, Ezelstraat 47–9, 8000 Bruges, www.snuffel.be

WHERE TO STAY

With more than 100 hotels throughout the city, Bruges has a wide range of establishments and locations. Hotels that are part of an international chain will provide a predictable degree of comfort, but guests may miss the more authentic Flemish hospitality offered by locally run establishments. It is always advisable to book in advance. Your first port of call should be the tourist office website, www.visitbruges.be – or www.visitgent.be. Bruges is particularly crowded in the summer, tending to be busiest at weekends.

Prices are based on the cost per night of a double room with en-suite bath or shower, including service charge, sales tax and breakfast. Rates can vary according to the season or time of the week. All the hotels listed here accept major credit cards.

€€€€	**above 320 euros**
€€€	**220–320 euros**
€€	**120–220 euros**
€	**below 120 euros**

BRUGES

Acacia €€ *Korte Zilverstraat 3A–5, 8000 Bruges*, www.hotel-acacia.com. This comfortable modern hotel is centrally located just off the Markt. All rooms have a private bathroom, television, minibar, telephone and safe; some have air conditioning. Has parking for 20 cars. A continental buffet breakfast is served every morning.

Bauhaus Budget Hotel € *Langestraat 133–7*, www.bauhaus.be. This decent low-cost hotel is close to the eastern ring canal park. Although it might not win many design awards, the rooms ranging in size from singles to quads, and an atmospheric bar-restaurant, are undoubted draws for the youthful clientele that shows up here.

Bourgoensche Cruyce €€ *Wollestraat 41–3, 8000 Bruges,* www.relais bourgondischcruyce.be. This is a tiny, charming wooden-fronted hotel (just

16 rooms) in a canalside location. Rooms are decorated in sumptuous 17th-century Flemish style with carved antique furniture, stone floors and large fireplaces. The hotel featured in the 2008 hit film *In Bruges*.

Bryghia €€ *Oosterlingenplein 4;* www.bryghiahotel.be. This friendly, family-run hotel is situated in a peaceful neighbourhood, rarely visited by tourists. Part of it occupies a 15th-century building that once belonged to Hanseatic merchants. The interior is cosy and tastefully furnished with comfortable sofas and wood beams. Some rooms enjoy a view of a quiet canal.

Cavalier € *Kuipersstraat 25, 8000 Bruges,* www.hotelcavalier.be. In spite of its slightly ramshackle external appearance, this small, two-star hotel (eight rooms) behind the city theatre is friendly and ordered and offers good value in the cheaper range of hotels.

Central € *Markt 30, 8000 Bruges,* www.hotelcentral.be. The name is entirely appropriate, since it would be hard to imagine a more central location in Bruges than on the Markt, directly facing the Belfry. This great-value small hotel has eight smart rooms, and there is a fine restaurant downstairs with a terrace on the square. Breakfast included.

Crowne Plaza Bruges €€€ *Burg 10, 8000 Bruges,* www.ihg.com. Centrally located deluxe hotel that's an intriguing blend of ancient and modern: the building incorporates the foundations of the demolished St Donatian's Cathedral, part of the 10th-century city wall and a 16th-century cellar. Bedrooms are well equipped (some have views of the historic Burg) and there is a pool and wellness centre.

De Orangerie €€€€ *Kartuizerinnenstraat 10, 8000 Bruges,* www.hotelorangerie.be. This luxurious hotel is wonderfully situated on the banks of the canal opposite Dijver. The rooms are all individually furnished, with lavish marble bathrooms. Breakfast on the canalside veranda on a warm summer morning is a real delight.

De Tuilerieen €€€ *Dijver 7, 8000 Bruges,* www.hoteltuilerieen.com. Situated just a few doors away from the main museums, this sumptuous hotel offers romantic-style rooms, some of which have views of the Dijver canal. Facilities include a pool, sauna, solarium and bar.

Die Swaene €€€ *Steenhouwersdijk 1, 8000 Bruges,* www.dieswaene.com. Award-winning romantic hotel with charming, attentive staff and rooms elegantly and individually furnished to a high standard. The lounge was originally the Guild Hall of the Tailors. Some of the rooms are in a separate wing, called the Canal House.

Duc de Bourgogne €€ *Huidenvettersplein 12, 8000 Bruges,* www.ducde bourgogne.be. This small hotel occupies an attractive step-gabled house in historic Huidenvettersplein (Tanners' Square), right in the heart of the city. The hotel is elegantly, if a little over-ornately, decorated, with lots of tapestries adorning the walls and lavish antique furniture.

Dukes' Palace €€€€ *Ontvangersstraat 9, 8000 Bruges,* www.dukespalace residence.com. This elegant hotel is traditionally furnished, with wood panelling, chandeliers and antiques; it also has excellent bathrooms. It has a warm atmosphere, and possibly the best breakfast in Bruges.

Fevery € *Collaert Mansionstraat 3, 8000 Bruges,* www.hotelfevery.be. A small, friendly family-run eco-hotel in an extremely quiet location just off Langerei, the long canal that reaches towards the north of the city. Bikes are available for hire.

Graaf van Vlaanderen € *'t Zand 19, 8000 Bruges,* www.graafvanlaanderen. be. A good budget choice, this small, family-run hotel has pleasant rooms, a bustling restaurant and tearoom, and a lively atmosphere emanating from the nightlife options on its doorstep.

Gulden Vlies €€ *Koningin Elisabethlaan 40, 8000 Brugge,* www.guldenvlies. be. Small family-run hotel with Art Deco touches outside and smart rooms inside. A 15-minute walk north of the centre.

Heritage €€ *Niklaas Desparsstraat 11, 8000 Bruges,* www.hotel-heritage.com. A hotel that delivers country-manor style within an old Bruges town house. The rooms are relatively small, but luxuriously appointed, and the breakfast room has a decorated ceiling with a chandelier. There is an excellent restaurant serving French-Flemish food.

Jan Brito €€ *Freren Fonteinstraat 1, 8000 Bruges,* www.janbrito.com/en. Creatively restored old mansion, full of period detail, plus a scattering of more modern rooms situated just a short walk away from the city's major attractions.

Lucca € *Naaldenstraat 30, 8000 Bruges,* www.hotellucca.be. Housed in a building that stands atop a 14th-century cellar once used by Italian traders from Lucca, this fine little hotel offers a lot of traditional atmosphere in its breakfast room and other public spaces, and plain character in the rooms.

Martin's Relais Oud Huis Amsterdam €€€€ *Genthof 4A, 8000 Bruges,* www.martinshotels.com/en. A rambling canalside building, parts of which date from the 14th century, are the setting for this fine hotel with large, ornate rooms. Those in the front have a canal view and those at the back look out onto a courtyard and garden. There is a wooden staircase, chandeliers and oak beams and a pretty interior courtyard.

Montanus €€ *Nieuwe Gentweg 76–8, 8000 Bruges,* www.montanus.be. Tasteful, restrained elegance in a historic house. In addition to the bedrooms in the main building, there are more modern and very well appointed rooms in the cottage-like structure at the back of the garden.

Navarra Brugge €€€ *Sint-Jakobsstraat 41, 8000 Bruges,* www.hotelnavarra.com. Housed in a mansion that used to be a royal residence in the 17th century – albeit 'only' of a prince – this thoroughly modernised hotel treats its guests like minor royalty. You can relax in the peaceful garden and kick back in the wellness centre.

NH Brugge €€€ *Boeveriestraat 2, 8000 Bruges,* www.nh-hotels.com. Large rooms and an atmospheric setting in a 17th-century monastery just off the bustling 't Zand Square add character to this large and well-equipped hotel, which has its own heated indoor swimming pool.

Rosenburg €€ *Coupure 30, 8000 Bruges,* www.rosenburg.be. A quiet hotel situated on the banks of a canal approximately a 10-minute walk from the centre of Bruges. The atmosphere in this modern brick building is relaxed and friendly, and staff are particularly helpful.

Ter Brughe €€ *Oost-Gistelhof 2, 8000 Bruges,* www.hotelterbrughe.com. Extremely attractive hotel in the elegant St Giles quarter, five minutes' walk from the centre of Bruges. Breakfast is served in the 14th-century beamed and vaulted cellar, which was once a warehouse for goods brought along the canal.

Ter Duinen €€ *Langerei 52, 8000 Bruges,* www.terduinenhotel.eu. This pleasant waterfront hotel set along the canal stretching northeast from the city centre offers a good compromise between essential facilities and cost, modern fittings and traditional looks.

Ter Reien €€ *Langestraat 1, 8000 Bruges,* www.hotelterreien.be. 'The Canals' hotel is an inexpensive option on the junction of two lovely canals, and occupies the house where the Symbolist painter Fernand Khnopff spent his childhood. All 26 rooms are bright and comfortable, although some have bathrooms which are very compact. They face the canal, courtyard or street, and prices reflect this. Breakfast can be taken in the pretty courtyard.

The Pand Hotel €€€ *Pandreitje 16, 8000 Bruges,* www.pandhotel.com. Old-fashioned furnishings complement modern conveniences and lend an authentic touch to the rooms in this quiet hotel set in an 18th-century mansion near the Markt. The excellent breakfasts are cooked on a cast-iron range in the breakfast room.

GHENT

Cour St-Georges Hotel €€ *Hoogpoort 75, 9000 Ghent,* www.hotel-courst georges.be. Most of the rooms at this hotel are actually in a modern, rather basic annexe situated across the road from the ancient building (originally the house used by the Guild of Crossbowmen), which dates back to 1228.

Flandria Hotel € *Barrestraat 3, 9000 Ghent,* www.flandriahotel.be/en. Inexpensive, basic 23-room hotel in a quiet side street close to the cathedral. Ideal for those on a shoestring budget looking only for a place to sleep, wash and change their clothes. Substantial breakfasts and friendly staff.

Ghent River Hotel €€€€ *Waaistraat 5,* www.ghent-river-hotel.be. This stylish waterfront hotel near the Vrijdagmarkt evokes the trading history of Ghent.

Some rooms occupy a restored 19th-century sugar factory, while others are in a 16th-century town house; the square was the site of a yarn market in the Middle Ages and the 19th century. When booking, ask for one of the rooms in the former factory, as these have oak beams, brick walls and odd industrial implements used for decoration. The rooms in the modern extension are plainer. The hotel has a rooftop breakfast room with striking views of the old city, a jetty and a fitness room.

Gravensteen €€ *Jan Breydelstraat 35, 9000 Ghent*, www.gravensteen.be. This 19th-century mansion, once the home of an industrial magnate, has been turned into one of the city's more elegant hotels. It is situated across footsteps from the Gravensteen castle, of which the rooms at the front have a fine view, and it has been tastefully renovated and extended. There is a fitness room and sauna.

Hotel Onderbergen €€ *Onderbergen 69, 9000 Ghent*, www.hotelonderbergen. be. Excellent-value boutique hotel a five-minute walk south of the centre. Rooms are spacious and feature hand-painted wallpaper.

Monasterium €€ *Oude Houtlei 56, 9000 Ghent*, www.monasterium.be. This converted 19th-century neo-Gothic convent offers standard modern rooms, as well as some simpler, cheaper rooms (**€**) in the adjoining Guesthouse PoortAckere. Located in what were formerly nuns' cells, these rooms are fairly basic, but ideal for budget travellers. Breakfast (extra charge) is served in an ornate refectory.

NH Gent-Belfort €€€ *Hoogpoort 63, 9000 Ghent*, www.nh-hotels.com. Superbly located opposite the Stadhuis, the Gent-Belfort offers excellent value for a hotel of this quality. The bright, lively rooms are well appointed and extremely comfortable, with splendid bathrooms. There is a fitness room and sauna.

INDEX

B

Basiliek van het Heilig-
    Bloed 30
Begijnhof 39
Bonne-Chièremolen 51
Brouwerij De Halve
    Maan 38
Brugse Vrije 31
Burg 28

C

Craenenburg 28

D

Damme 55
    De Grote Sterre 56
    Onze-Lieve-
        Vrouwekerk 57
    Sint-Janshospitaal 56
    Stadhuis 55
De Haan 58
    Grand Hotel Belle
        Vue 58
    Hotel Des Brasseurs 58
    Tramstation 58
    Villa Savoyarde 58
De Meulenaere 41
De Moor 44
Diamantmuseum Brugge 41
Dudzele 57
    Heemkundigmuseum
        De Groene Tente 57
    Sint-Pieters-
        Bandenkerk 57
Duinenabdij 53
Dumery-Klok 43

E

Engels Klooster Onze-
    Lieve-Vrouw van
    Nazareth 50
Ezelpoort 53

F

Flanders Fields 63
Frietmuseum 52

G

Gezellemuseum 51
Ghent 68
    Belfort 71
    Design Museum
        Gent 75
    De Zwane 74
    Dulle Griet 76
    Gildehuis van de
        Graanmeters 75
    Gildehuis van de
        Metselaars 75
    Gildehuis van de
        Onvrije Schippers 74
    Gildehuis van de Vrije
        Schippers 74
    Gravensteen 75
    Groot Vleeshuis 72
    Het Spijker 75
    Hotel d'Hane-
        Steenhuyse 77
    Huis der Gekroonde
        Hoofden 75
    Huis van Alijn 76
    Koninklijke Vlaamse
        Academie voor
        Taal 77
    Kouter 78
    Kunsthal Sint-
        Pietersabdij 81
    Lakenhalle 71
    Museum Arnold
        Vander Haeghen 78
    Museum of Industry,
        Work and Textile 77
    Museum voor Schone
        Kunsten 79
    Onze-Lieve-Vrouw
        Sint-Pieterskerk 81
    Sint-Baafskathedraal
        69
    Sint-Jorishof 72
    Sint-Michielskerk 73
    Sint-Niklaaskerk 72
    Stadhuis 71
    STAM 79
    Tolhuisje 75
    Tussen Bruggen 74
    Vrijdagmarkt 76
Gloribus 44
Godshuis De Pelikaanhuis
    32
Godshuis de Vos 40
Good Buys 84
Groeningemuseum 33
Gruuthusemuseum 35

H

Historium 27
Hof van Watervliet 42
Huidevettershuis 33
Huis Bouchoute 28

Huis De la Torre 47
Huis Ter Beurze 51

J
Jan van Eyckplein 46
Jeruzalemkapel 48

K
Kantcentrum 49
Kapucijnenkerk 43
Karmelietenkerk 53
Kasteel Loppem 67
Kasteel Minnewater 40
Kasteel Tillegem 67
Koninklijke Golf Club
    Oostende 59

L
Landhuis van het Brugse
    Vrije 31
Langemark 66
Lissewege 57
    Onze-Lieve-Vrouw-
        Bezoekingskerk 57

M
Markt 26
Minnewater 40
Minnewater Park 40

N
Natuurreservaat De
    Kijkuit 59
Nightlife 88

O
Onze-Lieve-Vrouwekerk 35
Onze-Lieve-Vrouw ter
    Potterie 53

Onze-Lieve-Vrouw-van-
    Blindekenskapel 44
Onze-Lieve-Vrouw van de
    Zeven Weeën 41
Onze-Lieve-Vrouw van
    Troost van Spermalie
    39
Oostende 59
    Amandine 60
    Casino-Kursaal 60
    Ensorhuis 60
    Koninklijke
        Gaanderijen 60
    Kunst Museum aan
        Zee 61
    Mercator 61
    Sint-Petrus-en-
        Pauluskerk 61
    Venetiaanse
        Gaanderijen 60
    Vistrap 60
Oosterlingenhuis 53
Oude Civiele Griffie 32
Oud Waterhuis 44

P
Poortersloge 47
Prinselijk Begijnhof ten
    Wijngaarde 39
Prinsenhof 45
Proosdij 28

R
restaurants
    Bistro Bruut 102
    Den Amand 103
    Den Gouden Harynck
        103
    De Karmeliet 105

De Schaar 103
Rozenhoedkaai 33

S
Sanctuary Wood Cemetery
    65
Schuttersgilde Sint-
    Joris 51
Schuttersgilde Sint-
    Sebastiaans 50
Simon Stevinplein 42
Sint-Andries suburb 67
    Domein Beisbroek 67
    Domein Tudor 67
Sint-Annakerk 48
Sint-Gilliskerk 54
Sint-Godelieve Abdij 43
Sint-Jakobskerk 52
Sint-Jan
    Nepomucenusbrug 33
Sint-Janshospitaal 37
Sint-Janshuismolen 51
Sint-Jozef 41
Sint-Salvators-kathedraal
    42
Sint-Walburgakerk 48
Smedenpoort 44
Speelmanskapel 45
Stadhuis 28
Stadspark Sebrechts 45
Sucx 44

T
Tillegembos 67
Tolhuis 47
Tyne Cot Commonwealth
    War Graves Cemetery
    66
't Zand 42

V
Van Campen 44
Van Peenen 44
Veurne 62
    Landhuis 63
    Sint-Niklaaskerk 63
    Sint-Walburgakerk 63
    Spaans Paviljoen 63
    Stadhuis 62

Vismarkt 32
Vladslo cemetery 67
Volkskundemuseum 50

W
Where to Shop 83

Y
Ypres 64

In Flanders Fields
    Museum 64
Menin Gate memorial
    64

Z
Zeebrugge 57
    Seafront Zeebrugge
    57

THE **MINI** ROUGH GUIDE TO
BRUGES & GHENT

First edition 2024

Editor: Beth Williams
Author: Phil Lee
Picture Editor: Tom Smyth
Cartography Update: Carte
Layout: Greg Madejak
Head of DTP and Pre-Press: Rebeka Davies
Head of Publishing: Sarah Clark
Photography Credits: Apa Publications 33;
Bruges Tourism 52; Dreamstime 82; Fotolia 48, 62,
65, 77; Glyn Genin/Apa Publications 26, 29, 31, 36,
37, 43, 45, 58, 73, 86, 87, 88, 93, 97; imageBROKER/
REX/Shutterstock 54; Inge Kinnet/Musea Brugge
4TC; iStock 20; iStockphoto 40, 47, 90; Musea
Brugge 68; Public domain 5M, 12, 15, 17, 34;
Shutterstock 1, 4MC, 4MC, 4TC, 4ML, 4TL, 4ML, 5T,
5M, 6T, 7T, 7B, 11, 24, 39, 50, 56, 61, 66, 71, 74, 79,
81, 85, 94, 98; Toerisme Brugge/Jan D'Hondt 91;
Tony Halliday/Apa Publications 19, 69
Cover Credits: Spiegelrei canal, Bruges
Shutterstock

Distribution
UK, Ireland and Europe: Apa Publications (UK)
Ltd; sales@roughguides.com
United States and Canada: Ingram Publisher
Services; ips@ingramcontent.com
Australia and New Zealand: Booktopia;
retailer@booktopia.com.au
Worldwide: Apa Publications (UK) Ltd;
sales@roughguides.com

**Special Sales, Content Licensing
and CoPublishing**
Rough Guides can be purchased in bulk
quantities at discounted prices. We can create
special editions, personalised jackets and
corporate imprints tailored to your needs.
sales@roughguides.com; http://roughguides.com

Contact us
Every effort has been made to provide accurate
information in this publication, but changes
are inevitable. The publisher cannot be held
responsible for any resulting loss, inconvenience
or injury sustained by any traveller as a result of
information or advice contained in the guide.
We would appreciate it if readers would call our
attention to any errors or outdated information,
or if you feel we've left something out. Please
send your comments with the subject line
"Rough Guide Mini Bruges & Ghent Update" to
mail@uk.roughguides.com.